Library
Canterbury High School
Ottawa

The Critical Idiom

Founder Editor: JOHN D. JUMP (1969–1976)

19 Rhetoric

In the same series

Rhetoric/*Peter Dixon*

Methuen & Co Ltd

First published 1971
by Methuen & Co Ltd
11 New Fetter Lane, London EC4P 4EE
Reprinted 1977

© 1971 Peter Dixon

Printed in Great Britain
by J. W. Arrowsmith Ltd, Bristol

ISBN 0 416 66760 0

This paperback edition is sold subject to the condition
that it shall not by way of trade or otherwise, be lent, resold,
hired out, or otherwise circulated without the publisher's prior
consent in any form of binding or cover other than
that in which it is published and without a similar
condition including this condition being imposed
on the subsequent purchaser.

Library
Canterbury High School
Ottawa

Distributed in the U.S.A. by
HARPER & ROW PUBLISHERS, INC.
BARNES & NOBLE IMPORT DIVISION

For PAUL, MICHAEL, *and* JANE
'insatiable in discourse'

———————————

Contents

General Editor's Preface

The volumes composing the Critical Idiom deal with a wide variety of key terms in our critical vocabulary. The purpose of the series differs from that served by the standard glossaries of literary terms. Many terms are adequately defined for the needs of students by the brief entries in these glossaries, and such terms do not call for attention in the present series. But there are other terms which cannot be made familiar by means of compact definitions. Students need to grow accustomed to them through simple and straightforward but reasonably full discussions. The main purpose of this series is to provide such discussions.

Many critics have borrowed methods and criteria from currently influential bodies of knowledge or belief that have developed without particular reference to literature. In our own century, some of them have drawn on art-history, psychology, or sociology. Others, strong in a comprehensive faith, have looked at literature and literary criticism from a Marxist or a Christian or some other sharply defined point of view. The result has been the importation into literary criticism of terms from the vocabularies of these sciences and creeds. Discussions of such bodies of knowledge and belief in their bearing upon literature and literary criticism form a natural extension of the initial aim of the Critical Idiom.

Because of their diversity of subject-matter, the studies in the series vary considerably in structure. But all authors have tried to give as full illustrative quotation as possible, to make reference whenever appropriate to more than one literature, and to write in such a way as to guide readers towards the short bibliographies in which they have made suggestions for further reading.

University of Manchester   John D. Jump

Note

Apart from a few key words and phrases in the original Greek or Latin, quotations from classical authors are given in translation only, for reasons of space. The translations used, unless otherwise stated, are those in the Loeb Classical Library series.

I

Introduction:
Some Modern Instances

In his essay '"Rhetoric" and Poetic Drama' T. S. Eliot outlined a difficult task. Rhetoric, he said, 'is one of those words which it is the business of criticism to dissect and reassemble' (*Selected Essays*, p. 38). The critic may perhaps be excused for feeling that he is in the position of a man trying to dissect and reassemble a jellyfish – for the word, as Eliot went on to acknowledge, is notoriously slippery and imprecise. It has served to designate a number of radically different stylistic qualities. It has been invoked in order to praise writers, and at other times in order to condemn. So invertebrate is the word that we can apparently turn it inside out. Etymologically the *rhetor* (ῥήτωρ) is a public speaker, and his distinctive art is that of addressing courts of law and popular assemblies. Yet when the judges in a recent debating competition laid down guidelines for the competitors they 'advised against rhetoric' (*The Observer*, 26 January 1969). Cicero and Quintilian would have found such advice incomprehensible.

We may be able to reduce some of this confusion to a semblance of order by drawing out the implications of the word's etymology. To speak in public presupposes an audience which is spoken to, an audience which the speaker wishes to influence, to persuade, perhaps to exhort and instruct. And public speech is necessarily different from private chat. The *rhetor* will use more artistic, more artificial and formal kinds of language than he would in everyday conversation. At the very least he will be more orderly than usual, choosing his words with greater precision; otherwise he may find himself not communicating to an audience but addressing the empty air. If, then, out of these implications we construct a working definition of *rhetor* – 'a man skilled in speaking who addresses a public audience in order to make an impact upon it' – we may begin to see how the diverse uses of the word *rhetoric* in modern criticism can be traced back through various historical diversions and intersections to the several components of this basic definition.

Everything depends on the element which is stressed or isolated. T. S. Eliot, for instance, focuses on the public aspect of the speaker's art. 'The really fine rhetoric of Shakespeare occurs in situations where a character in the play *sees himself* in a dramatic light' (p. 39). The character, that is, deliberately assumes a public stance, as in Othello's final speech: 'And say besides, that in Aleppo once. . . .' Keeping the same basic emphasis, but extending its application, the critic may describe as rhetorical any literary work which is evidently intended for the public ear, and which has the tone and manner of a man speaking to a wide audience on some theme or subject of general importance. Taken in this sense rhetoric stands in contrast to a more intimate or private communing with the reader. So W. W. Robson writes of Byron's description of the dying gladiator in *Childe Harold's Pilgrimage*: 'This of course is rhetorical writing, but it is a very distinguished rhetoric. . . . Byron speaks here in the accents of a great European tradition of the public style' (*Critical Essays*, London, 1966, pp. 156–7).

If we next lay particular stress on that part of our definition which concerns the speaker's impact on his listeners, then we can stretch rhetoric to include almost the entire area of human discourse, since most of our speech and writing (even much of our soliloquizing) is directed to an audience, however small. The concern of rhetoric becomes nothing less than the whole complex business of communication through language, the intricate network of relationships which connects a speaker (or writer) with those he addresses. Thus I. A. Richards re-defines rhetoric as the 'study of verbal understanding and misunderstanding' (*Philosophy of Rhetoric*, p. 23). Here too belong the courses in Rhetoric and Composition given in American high schools and universities, which aim to teach proficiency in communication, more especially in the writing of clear expository prose. Such courses will often include exercises in 'straight thinking' and practice in the marshalling of arguments, so that rhetoric has recaptured some of the ground it earlier lost to logic. Finally, as a literary-critical term, rhetoric in this sense will cover all the techniques by which a writer establishes rapport with his readers, and by which he elicits and guides their responses to his work. It is thus that the word is used in Wayne C. Booth's *The Rhetoric of Fiction*, a detailed study of 'the author's means of controlling his readers' (Preface).

In the uses of the term that we have so far surveyed, something of the third component of our working definition is already present: the element of artifice and ingenuity, of language polished or heightened beyond what we loosely call our 'normal' habits of speech. By emphasizing this element we arrive at a new meaning of rhetoric: the art of speaking well, of using words to their best advantage. Since poetry has customarily been regarded as the field in which words are handled with their maximum force and expressiveness, we find that the links between rhetoric and poetry have been numerous and firm, at least until the conception of poetry as a verbal craft began to fall into discredit. Indeed the two arts of language have sometimes been treated as though they were one. Our awareness of this historical state of affairs has encouraged the continuing use of *rhetoric* as a synonym for *poetry*, as when a reviewer comments on a recent study of Pope: 'Throwing more light on certain selected scientific interests of the period than on Pope's poetry, its actual centre of concern is not rhetoric but the history of ideas' (Rebecca Parkin, in *Eighteenth-Century Studies*, III (1969–70), p. 139). More commonly, rhetoric is taken to refer specifically to tropes and figures of speech, those graces of style and patterns of words which most obviously display an author's verbal skill and resourcefulness. So, in 'The Rhetoric of *Brunanburh*' Ann S. Johnson examines the 'embellished verbal figures' (the 'rhetoric' of her title) in that Old English heroic poem, and concludes that the anonymous poet had absorbed at least some of the forms and devices of classical rhetoric (*Philological Quarterly*, XLVII (1968), pp. 487–93).

Teachers and exponents of rhetoric have repeatedly claimed that since speech is man's great privilege, distinguishing him from the beasts, their art is of central relevance to human affairs. The price it pays for such relevance is to become enmeshed in moral issues, value-judgments, questions of good and evil. These problems our neutral description has so far ignored. We are now presented with a further set of possible meanings for rhetoric, depending on our assessment of the orator's moral character and the ends to which his verbal dexterity is directed. If we make a positive moral commitment and assert that the orator is 'a *good* man, skilled in speaking', we are in fact echoing Cato's definition: *vir bonus dicendi peritus*. The classical champions of rhetoric were unshaken in their adherence to this definition, in their conviction that goodness is a prerequisite of the true orator. But their very firmness is an attempt to disguise an underlying anxiety; it obliquely testifies to the existence of a counter-definition – that the orator is quite as likely to be a wicked man, manipulating his hearers for evil purposes. Even more damagingly, the whole art of rhetoric may be censured as morally reprehensible, the view taken by Socrates, its first and most formidable opponent.

During the long history of rhetoric the rumblings of moral disapproval have often dwindled to the merest whisper. But as the result of profound intellectual, social, and political changes which began in Europe in the seventeenth century, the dissatisfaction has grown steadily in volume and has even threatened to drown the voice of true rhetoric altogether. By the early years of the present century, as Eliot noted, *rhetoric* had become 'merely a vague term of abuse for any style that is bad, that is so evidently bad or second rate that we do not recognize the necessity for greater precision in the phrases we apply to it' (*Selected Essays*, p. 37). Rhetoric is a convenient label for all the most trivial and unworthy ways of attempting to move or influence an audience. To be more exact, it may refer to a literary style that clamours for us to admire its virtuosity, a style of tinsel ornament, meretricious show without substance. Or it can be applied to the style that tries to impress by taking the easy way of over-emphasis, the way which leads to fustian, rant and bombast. So J. M. S. Tompkins comments on a minor eighteenth-century novel, Sophia King's *Waldorf*: 'The calamities of this story are heaped up by the unsparing hand of youth, and described in distressing rhetoric', and quotes a nice example of the author's absurd exaggeration: 'The eyes of Waldorf seemed bursting with the majestic energy of intellect' (*The Popular Novel in England, 1770–1800*, London, 1932, p. 326). Or an author may hope to move us by a series of crudely sensational or sentimental appeals – a complaint which F. R. Leavis levels at *Le Père Goriot*: 'Balzac's art here seems to me an essentially rhetorical art in a pejorative sense of the adjective: romantic rhetoric is the life and spirit of the sublimities and degradations he exhibits. They depend for their effect, that is, not on any profound realization of human emotions, but on excited emphasis, top-level assertion and explicit insistence' (*The Great Tradition*, London, 1948, p. 29). Finally, by pushing our disapproval even further, we may come to dismiss as 'rhetorical' all empty, insincere declarations and the kind of cheap scoring of points which the judges in the debating contest presumably wished to avoid.

The inadmissibility of rhetoric is one of the rules of the question game played by Rosencrantz and Guildenstern:

GUILDENSTERN: What in God's name is going on?
ROSENCRANTZ: Foul! No rhetoric. Two-one.

(Tom Stoppard, *Rosencrantz and Guildenstern are Dead*,
London, 1967, p. 31)

But we cannot allow Rosencrantz to have the last word. The fortunes and the meaning of rhetoric are still fluctuating. In the chapters which follow I have attempted to record some of the major fluctuations of the past, and to indicate some of the ways in which rhetoric has impinged upon literature. I have also tried to suggest the scope of a subject that has made itself responsible not only for the examination of legal arguments and the minutiae of style, but also for the liberal education of kings and statesmen.

2

Classical Theory

The people of Athens made yearly sacrifices to the statue of the goddess Persuasion, whose worship was said to have been established in the city by Theseus. The sacrifices gave public and formal expression to the citizens' delight in discourse, and in the forcefulness of ideas persuasively presented. The power of words to move men's minds and influence their actions had for the Greeks something of magical and divine about it. This faith in the word has been sustained in Western civilization – it is not too much to say that it has been a sustaining force in Western civilization – in spite of receiving some very shrewd blows. Throughout Greek and Roman antiquity the practitioners and theorists of rhetoric, those at least who held a lofty conception of their role and their art, were concerned to affirm this faith directly, and to reaffirm it continually.

This sense of the efficacy of the spoken word is much older than the formal study and codification of the art of rhetoric. The heroes of Homer's epics acknowledge and exploit the power of speech, treasuring eloquence as one of the greatest of human excellences. It was not, however, until the fifth century B.C., among the Greek inhabitants of Sicily, that rhetoric as a distinct art was born. At that time landowners and others who had suffered under the recently expelled tyrants began civil proceedings to recover their rights. The Sicilians, reputedly a sharpwitted people and not averse to controversy, enlisted the help of Corax and Tisias in presenting their case. These two men were the first to 'put together some theoretical precepts'; before this time, 'while many had taken pains to speak with care and with orderly arrangement, no one had followed a definite method or art' (Cicero, *Brutus*, 46). The rhetorician is then, to begin with, the man who can advise on the most effective way of presenting a legal case. Corax is credited with the first Art of Rhetoric, and with the first extant definition of the word: πειθοῦς δημιουργός (artificer, or producer, of persuasion). Rhetoric was soon to be extended beyond legal and political occasions, to situations in which persuasion, narrowly considered, was not a prime motive of the speaker; yet the persuasive or influential aim, inevitable in the setting of the law court, has never been quite lost sight of. Indeed, at Rome the study of rhetoric was often restricted to legal contexts, and both Cicero and Quintilian were keenly aware of the judicial functions of oratory.

The Sicilian Tisias is said to have taught Gorgias, who was in turn responsible for introducing oratory into Greece when he visited Athens as an ambassador. Gorgias specialized in writing set speeches in praise or censure of specific subjects or persons, thus widening the scope of the art (*Brutus*, 47). He laid particular stress on the decorative functions of style, favouring unusual phraseology and neologisms, and developed the kind of highly patterned prose which is most clearly represented in English literature by the writings of John Lyly. Most important, Gorgias and other teachers of rhetoric asserted that a speaker need not concern himself with the truth of the matter in hand. The rightness or wisdom of the cause is an irrelevance. What is important is simply the orator's verbal dexterity in putting across his conclusions in a convincing way. The teacher will therefore get his pupils to exercise their wits by preparing speeches on either side of a question without regard to the morality and wisdom of the point of view expressed. And it will not be long before such a teacher is advertising his ability to instruct pupils how to make the worse, or weaker, cause appear the better and stronger.

It was against such moral irresponsibility that Isocrates set himself, claiming for rhetoric a role higher and nobler than that of mere persuasion. Speech, Isocrates reminds us (and the idea has become a commonplace of Western thought), is the foundation of human society, the means through which man expresses his wisdom, and without which wisdom is inarticulate and inert. Presumably because of the bad name rhetoric was already getting, and as a result of his own impatience with the frivolous attitudes of his teachers (including, probably, Gorgias himself), Isocrates declared his concern to be the study and teaching, not of rhetoric, but of the 'art of speech' (ἡ τῶν λόγων παιδεία). This is an art requiring a vigorous and imaginative mind, for the *logos* embraces all aspects of communication. It comprehends reason, feeling and imagination, as well as the forms of expression; it is the power by which we direct public affairs, by which we influence others in the course of our daily lives, and by which we reach decisions about our own moral conduct. Isocrates writes to Alexander the Great, commending his devotion to this broadly conceived rhetorical training: 'By means of this study you will come to know how at the present time to form reasonably sound opinions about the future, how not ineptly to instruct your subject peoples what each should do, how to form correct judgments about the right and the just and their opposites and, besides, to reward and chastise each class as it deserves.' Isocrates argues that 'the power to speak well is taken as the surest index of a sound understanding, and discourse which is true and lawful and just is the outward image of a good and faithful soul' (*Nicocles*, 7: repeated in *Antidosis*, 255). Educationally, study of the *logos* will promote morality, since men can become more virtuous by conceiving 'an ambition to speak well' (*Antidosis*, 275). Speaking and writing on noble themes will enlarge the mind. Moreover, the orator must be a good man, and must be known to be so: 'words carry greater conviction when spoken by men of good repute.' The product of Isocrates' educational system will be a philosopher and statesman, one who

B

can mould public opinion by his speeches or writings, one who will always act justly and wisely. He is the embodiment of what Isocrates understood by *logos*: eloquent wisdom. This Isocratean ideal, transmitted by Cicero, was inherited by the Renaissance. Isocrates himself was admired by the humanist Ascham, and at the end of the sixteenth century his works were a regular part of the English grammar school curriculum. Milton venerated the 'old man eloquent' for practising the moral wisdom which he taught, and his own *Areopagitica*, in its title, its literary form – that of the 'written speech' – and its passionate concern with liberty, quite deliberately recalls Isocrates' *Areopagiticus*.

The relationship of means to ends, the possibility of skills and techniques being put to dishonest uses, has always been the most vulnerable aspect of rhetorical theory. It was at this point that Socrates directed his attack, forcing wide open the breach that Isocrates had tried to heal. Two of Plato's Socratic dialogues address themselves to the subject of rhetoric: the early *Gorgias* (written probably not long after the death of Socrates in 399 B.C.), and the later and much better known *Phaedrus* (about 370 B.C.). Between them these dialogues offer a penetrating critique of current theory and practice, a redefinition of rhetoric, a model speech (the famous discourse on love in the *Phaedrus*) and an assertion of the primacy of wisdom and truth over verbal skill. Eloquence and wisdom are no longer equal partners in the *logos*; wisdom is pre-eminent. Unless a man pays due attention to philosophy 'he will never be able to speak properly about anything' (*Phaedrus*, 261A). 'A real art of speaking . . . which does not seize hold of truth, does not exist and never will' (260E). And truth is to be pursued and seized, not by way of pleadings and set speeches, but by the method of dialectic, of question and answer, by the free play of the inquiring mind. Since, for Socrates, virtue is knowledge, all man's intellectual effort must be bent and directed towards knowing the truth.

The *Gorgias* aims to demolish the conventions of rhetorical theory by exposing their shallowness and inconsistency. Gorgias clings to the received idea that the orator is morally good, and his art morally sound. Yet he is forced to admit that rhetoric can be abused: a criminal can be defended skilfully, even successfully, by a lawyer who knows him to be a criminal, and an orator can prepare a speech advocating a course of action which he feels to be wrong. How, asks Socrates, can a just man thus use his art for unjust purposes? The rhetorician, it soon appears, is not seriously concerned with truth. His vaunted art is a device for persuading, an instrument of deception, a knack of producing easy gratification. It is a species of flattery, because it aims not at upholding the good but at falsifying reality in order to please. As cookery is to medicine, in relation to the health of the body, so is rhetoric to justice (465c). If rhetoric could approach to the condition of medicine, it would merit serious consideration. Its business would then be to point to what is just, to expose what is baneful and evil, so as to promote the moral health of the individual and the community. But such a rhetoric, which rigorously endeavours 'to make the citizens' souls as good as possible', and always says what is best, 'whether it prove more or less pleasant to one's hearers . . . is a rhetoric you never yet saw' (503A–B).

The dramatic context of the dialogue contributes powerfully to its argument. As it opens we learn that Gorgias has just concluded an oratorical performance, a brilliant virtuoso display, but one that obviously seeks to catch the applause of his friends and followers without aiming at any public or private good. His disciple Polus, who attempts to rebut Socrates when Gorgias retires from the somewhat unequal combat, displays the shoddy debating tricks of his trade. He attempts to laugh down an argument, and believes that witnesses should be assessed according to quantity rather than moral quality. In these ways the exponents of rhetoric are made to condemn themselves. In the later dialogue the case is even worse.

Socrates' friend, Phaedrus, has been impressed by a speech delivered by Lysias on the subject of love, and is induced to repeat this discourse, a piece of rhetorical bravura, for Socrates' benefit. On this showing Lysias cannot even construct a proper speech. He repeats himself and fails to define his terms. Socrates is led to enunciate two basic principles, of great importance for later practice: first, the orator should offer a preliminary definition of the nature of his topic, so as to give clarity and consistency to the whole speech; secondly he should carefully divide the subject into its component parts. The resulting speech will not be a mechanical assembly of points, for 'every discourse must be organized, like a living being, with a body of its own, as it were, so as not to be headless or footless, but to have a middle and members, composed in fitting relation to each other and to the whole' (264C). This ideal of organic unity, of completeness and proportion, is one which most subsequent theorists would gladly adopt.

Socrates, however, is not after all content to leave the rhetoricians in possession of this method and this ideal. For definition and division are the province not of rhetoric but of dialectic, the uncompromising search for truth, and unless rhetoric is firmly subordinated to dialectic it is worthless or worse. Lysias' speech is a conceited exercise in ingenuity, lacking even a pretence of conviction, and failing to carry out its heartless task with any proper care. Socrates reveals its technical shortcomings with a speech of his own on the same topic, better constructed, more clearly organized, but still evidently insincere. A skill so indifferent to truth and morality is, in Socrates' eyes, unworthy to be called an art: 'For whether one be awake or asleep, ignorance of right and wrong and good and bad is in truth inevitably a disgrace, even if the whole mob applaud it' (277D–E). To speak with a knowledge of the truth, but with the intention of leading your hearers away from it, for amusement's sake (as in Socrates' 'reply' to Lysias), is to be shameless and irresponsibly flippant. To seek the truth humbly but confidently, as in his second speech, which explores the nature of love and the soul, is to be not a rhetorician but a philosopher. This is why Isocrates alone among contemporary rhetoricians can be applauded. Nature has implanted a love of wisdom in his mind; he will not rest satisfied with oratorical expertise, for 'a more divine impulse will lead him to greater things' (279A). Wisdom is the beginning and end of eloquence.

There is one further objection that Socrates raises. Rhetoricians were already in the habit of writing speeches, either for their clients to deliver or as an alternative to delivering orations in public themselves. The fixity of the written word is for Socrates an obstacle in the path of truth, since the pursuit of wisdom depends on the free play of mind which the Socratic dialogue so triumphantly displays. Phaedrus has committed Lysias' tricked-out speech to his writing-tablets. That can teach him nothing, whereas his conversation with Socrates, we may conclude, has been really 'written in [his] soul' (278A). So the true end of rhetoric has been accomplished, and Socrates has answered in the affirmative his own earlier question: 'Is not rhetoric in its entire nature an art which leads the soul by means of words, not only in law courts and the various other public assemblages, but in private companies as well?' (261A).

In his penetrating and amusing way Socrates made fundamental criticisms that have been repeated both by antagonists of rhetoric and by literary theorists. No subsequent account of the subject, if it was to be anything more than superficial, could ignore his redefinition of it, and his relegating it to a status inferior to that of dialectic. Aristotle, a former pupil of Plato, certainly keeps the Socratic arguments clearly in mind in the 'Art' or manual of rhetoric which he composed about 330 B.C., and which is the only one of his several works on this subject to have survived. Its opening sentence quietly contradicts the principal Socratic argument. 'Rhetoric is a counterpart [ἀντίστροφος] of Dialectic'; the two studies fit together as the two halves of a whole, and the one is the legitimate equal of the other. Aristotle seeks to show that rhetoric has its own kind of intellectual rigour, no less than logic. By neglecting discipline, by making rhetoric appear soft and effeminate, previous writers had left themselves and their subject open to scorn. So Aristotle devotes considerable space to the ways in which the pleader can prove his case, and to a detailed study of the *enthymeme*, the orator's equivalent of the logician's syllogism. (Briefly, an enthymeme is an argument based on generally true or probable – as opposed to certain – premises, and leading to a particular, not a general, conclusion. For example: 'No man who is sensible ought to have his children taught to be excessively clever, for, not to speak of the charge of idleness brought against them, they earn jealous hostility from the citizens': Aristotle, *Rhetoric*, II. xxi. 2.) The effect is to emphasize that rhetoric is primarily a technique of argument, like dialectic, rather than of ornamentation.

Aristotle conducts the defence of rhetoric with great subtlety. His tactics include the offering of a new and refined definition. The function of rhetoric is not so much to persuade as to discover 'in each case the existing means of persuasion' (I. i. 14), selecting the best means from among those available and appropriate. This at once removes rhetoric from the realm of the haphazard and the fanciful. It also means that failure to persuade in any particular instance does not invalidate the entire art. Aristotle draws an analogy from medicine, no doubt with a knowing backward glance at Socrates' unflattering argument about medicine and cookery. Strictly speaking, the function of medical skill is not to restore the patient to health, but only to seek to promote that end; medicine does not lose its name and standing if a physician fails to cure the incurable. In contrast to the Socratic or Platonic search for an ideal rhetoric, Aristotle concerns himself with what rhetoric in practice actually is. If truth and justice are naturally superior to their opposites, and yet wrong decisions can be made (as they manifestly can) in assemblies and courts of law, then the responsibility must lie at least in part with the advocate of justice and truth. In other words, such an advocate must be no bungler. It is his moral duty to present his argument in the most efficacious way, and his task is too important to be left to chance and rule-of-thumb. (This is a doctrine which was to have important literary consequences in the Renaissance.) Aristotle stresses the practical value of rhetoric by suggesting that it may function as a kind of verbal self-defence – and we do not think any the worse of a man for attempting to defend himself against physical violence. Finally, to the Socratic argument that the irresponsible use of the faculty of speech may do grave harm, it may be replied that all good things (strength or military skill, for example) may be abused; only virtue itself is safe.

We can see that Aristotle is anxious to clear the name of rhetoric. He is at times somewhat defensive, always practical and instructive, insisting on intellectual discipline and the need for the orator to take pains. It was for Cicero to reinstate oratory on its lofty, Isocratean pedestal, to proclaim that man touches his highest excellence in his devotion to the ideal of eloquent wisdom. Cicero's own life was certainly devoted to this ideal. His philosophical and moral treatises discuss topics of general and continuing importance – friendship, old age, man's social duties – and were for centuries esteemed as storehouses of practical wisdom. George Puttenham declared that Cicero was the wisest of all the Roman authors (*Arte of English Poesie*, p. 292). As an orator and pleader he was eminently successful. His writings on rhetoric range from the youthful and derivative *De Inventione* ('On Invention'), through the long and elaborate *De Oratore* ('Concerning the Orator'), to the *Brutus* (a history of Roman oratory) and the *Orator*, both composed some three years before his death.

Finally, he sacrificed first his career and then his life in the cause of freedom of speech. It is not surprising that during the Renaissance Cicero and rhetoric should be synonymous. His noble enthusiasm for oratory, expressed in the works of his middle and later years, is solidly founded on actual practice. He spoke from the fullness of experience when he declared that 'there is nothing that has so potent an effect upon human emotions as well-ordered and embellished speech' (*Brutus*, 193). So he could feel free to put Socrates firmly in his place. The fissure which Socrates thought he perceived between intellectual truth – the genuine end of oratory – and a graceful but possibly deceptive means of presentation, was a fissure of his own making: 'Socrates . . . in his discussions separated the science of wise thinking from that of elegant speaking, though in reality they are closely linked together. . . . This is the source from which has sprung the undoubtedly absurd and unprofitable and reprehensible severance between the tongue and the brain, leading to our having one set of professors to teach us to think and another to teach us to speak' (*De Oratore*, III. 60–1). Cicero acknowledges that no one can be a good speaker who is not also a sound thinker (*Brutus*, 23). What he demands is that speaking and thinking should be closely united, not set at odds. He appeals to pre-Socratic traditions: 'the older masters down to Socrates used to combine with their theory of rhetoric the whole of the study and the science of everything that concerns morals and conduct and ethics and politics' (*De Oratore*, III. 72). And Aristotle is praised for pioneering the return to a condition of unity, since he endeavoured to join 'the scientific study of facts with practice in style' (III. xxxv. 141).

Cicero does not face squarely the issue of moral irresponsibility. Neither does he confront the Socratic arguments with the Aristotelian ones. Instead his case turns on the point that 'wise thinking' and 'elegant speaking' are closely linked because thought, the subject-matter or material of speech (the *res*), is inseparable from the words (*verba*) in which it is made manifest. Expression and thought are indivisible. We cannot properly talk of expressing a thought in different words, for it will become a different (even if only a slightly different) thought in the process. Cicero, in fact, does not rigidly or consistently hold this view, nor, as Quintilian perceived, can some other parts of his rhetorical theory be squared with it. But it does have interesting consequences for his programme of rhetorical education. Cicero would not set students exercises in paraphrase, because this would create a false conception of the relationship between *res* and *verba*, encouraging the notion that verbal re-formulation does not affect the sense. On the other hand exercise in translation (say, from Greek into Latin) would tend to foster the sense of that relationship. The student has to grasp the thought-word unit in its totality, and to render that unit as completely as the other language will allow.

Cicero's call is for synthesis, the union of *res* and *verba*, of thinking and speaking, of ethics and style. For him, as for Isocrates, the perfect orator possesses 'wisdom combined with eloquence' (*De Oratore*, III. 142). Such a man will fulfil himself in public life and public leadership, in exactly the kind of civic responsibility which was distasteful to Socrates, whose reluctance to enter the political arena is frowned on by Cicero. The Ciceronian orator may properly be called a philosopher. But if there are those who still insist on distinguishing these two roles and on estimating their relative values, then Cicero is ready with his own firm assessment: 'the consummate orator possesses all the knowledge of the philosophers, but the range of philosophers does not necessarily include eloquence; and although they look down on it, it cannot but be deemed to add a crowning embellishment to their sciences' (*De Oratore*, III. 143). An education in oratory is a complete education. Besides providing a valuable mental discipline, it is a pleasure and a good in itself. In the treatise which bears his name Marcus Brutus testifies that 'so far as eloquence is concerned, my pleasure is not so much in its rewards and the renown that it confers, as in the study and training which it involves' (*Brutus*, 23).

Quintilian shared this view of the major, integrating role which rhetoric must play in any educational system. His *Institutio Oratoria* ('The Education of an Orator'), written towards the end of the first century A.D., defines and establishes this role with great thoroughness, giving particular weight to the conjunction of ethics and eloquence. He declares at the outset that the first essential for the perfect orator is that he should be a good man (Book I. pref. 9 ff.). In a sense his whole treatise is an expansion of Cato's definition of the orator: *vir bonus dicendi peritus*. Time and time again he reminds his readers that the moral character of the speaker must inform the whole speech, and at the opening of his final Book he states the principle in its most uncompromising form: 'I do not merely assert that the ideal orator should be a good man, but I affirm that no man can be an orator unless he is a good man' (XII. i. 3). We may regret that the Ciceronian wisdom has been narrowed into moral character, but the conception of oratory is still a lofty one. At the same time Quintilian displays that practical turn of mind which Horace saw as distinctively Roman. There is much sound and detailed advice in the specifically educational sections of the work, and an intense concern throughout with details of language and aspects of usage. This may reveal itself either in the refutation of received ideas about the nature of language, as when he declares that 'there is no word which is intrinsically ugly unless it be beneath the dignity of the subject on which we have to speak, excepting always such words as are nakedly obscene' (VIII. iii. 38); or in crisp summary of earlier rhetorical doctrine: 'it is in verbs that the real strength of language resides' (IX. iv. 26) – a dictum which modern critics have not overlooked.

Of necessity Quintilian goes over much of the Ciceronian ground, though he frequently takes an independent line. A major area of disagreement concerns the relationship of *res* to *verba*.

Quintilian sees that Cicero's belief in indivisibility of thought and word is difficult to reconcile with the theory of *decorum*, the suiting of style to matter, which is a doctrine that Cicero also strenuously upholds. If we can talk of suitability, but perhaps especially if we can talk of unsuitability, then we are thinking in terms of a relationship between words and thought, not of a unity. In Quintilian's view, words can express thoughts either more or less adequately. He would consider it meaningful and precise to say that the same thought has been expressed obscurely by one speaker but clearly by another, or diffusely by one writer and elegantly by a second. 'For the same things are often put in different ways and the sense remains unaltered though the words are changed' (IX. i. 16). Educationally, this means that paraphrase *is* a valuable exercise. In discussing these matters Quintilian uses a metaphor which was to become standard: language as the dress of thought. If the expression of an idea seems unsatisfactory this may be because the garment of words is too skimpy or hangs too loosely. Again, the dress may look absurdly incongruous – or be intentionally so, as in burlesque, where the bumpkin wears finery and Venus is apparelled like a fishwife. In the best oratory the subject-matter will seem to have suggested, naturally and without strain, the words in which it is clothed (VIII. pref. 21). Or, looking at such a speech from another angle, we may say that the words are being used with the maximum of significance and fullness of meaning (VIII. ii. 9); the words fit the sense perfectly. We know that the clothes and their wearer are different entities; however, since the clothes suit the wearer and reveal his character we no longer think of them as distinct but rather apprehend and judge them as a totality.

In spite of quarrels with his great predecessor, Quintilian is clearly in the tradition which goes back through Cicero to Isocrates, and which holds that rhetoric provides a training for the whole man, that its end product is the wise and virtuous statesman, and that oratory is a powerful force for good when it is entrusted to responsible hands. Men are touched and moved to virtue by the spoken word, but the word must be spoken by virtuous men, and men moreover of skill and learning. 'Wherefore,' says Quintilian, 'let us seek with all our hearts that true majesty of oratory, the fairest gift of god to man, without which all things are stricken dumb and robbed alike of present glory and the immortal record of posterity; and let us press forward to whatsoever is best . . .' (XII. xi. 30).

3
The Rules of Rhetoric

No mention has so far been made of the treatise on rhetoric which enjoyed most popularity in the Middle Ages and early Renaissance. This was the anonymous *Rhetorica ad C. Herennium* ('Rhetoric addressed to Gaius Herennius'), composed about 85 B.C., and until the late fifteenth century confidently ascribed to Cicero. Even after this ascription had been challenged the work lingered in the Ciceronian canon, and in part derived its prestige from his name. But only in part. Something is also due to the fact that other authors were either incompletely known, or disregarded: Quintilian fell into the first category and Aristotle, at least as rhetorician, into the second. Moreover, though the *Ad Herennium* makes no contribution to rhetorical theory it is an excellent compendium of rhetorical practice, and possesses all the merits of a popular text-book. It is brisk, matter-of-fact, and clearly arranged. Its illustrative examples are full and appropriate; and by limiting the theory of rhetoric quite specifically to 'a set of rules that provide a definite method and system of speaking' (I. ii. 3) it immediately commends itself as the rhetorician's *vade mecum*. If it lacks the lofty idealism of Cicero, the subtlety of Aristotle, the linguistic insights of Quintilian, it fares none the worse as a popular manual.

Though written in Latin the *Ad Herennium* is a statement of Hellenistic practice, and a reflection of the Greek emphasis on judicial oratory. It is a vital link in the chain of rhetorical continuity. Its terminology and classifications, combined with those of Cicero's *De Inventione* (written a little earlier), were accepted as standard during the Middle Ages and influenced many later authors. In summarizing the doctrines of classical rhetoric I have followed these two authorities quite closely, while to illustrate the persistence of basic ideas, and the modification of details, I have drawn freely upon two English works, as being both representative and influential: Thomas Wilson's *Arte of Rhetorique*, first published in 1553, and Hugh Blair's *Lectures on Rhetoric and Belles Lettres*, published in 1783 but based on courses which Blair had begun in Edinburgh some twenty-four years earlier. Blair was highly esteemed in England during the nineteenth century, and in the United States, at least until about 1880, he was 'the accepted rhetorical teacher' (Croll, *Style, Rhetoric, and Rhythm*, p. 294).

THE THREE TYPES OF RHETORIC

Rhetoric may be categorized according to the cause or subject which the speaker is called upon to treat, and the role of the audience.

(i) *Judicial or forensic rhetoric* is the oratory of the law courts, the rhetoric of legal prosecution and defence. Whatever the facts of the individual case, the speaker's ultimate concern is with justice, and his hearers are required to reach a verdict about certain events in the past. The speaker will try to make the court well disposed towards himself and his client, but his main business is the statement of proof and the examination of evidence. Teachers of rhetoric from Aristotle to Quintilian pay most attention to the needs of this branch of oratory.

(ii) *Deliberative rhetoric* originated in popular and political assemblies. The speaker's task is to persuade or dissuade his hearers in relation to a course of action or decision of policy, and the role of the audience is now, in Aristotle's phrase, that of a 'judge of things to come'. In the Middle Ages the field of deliberative oratory was chiefly occupied by preachers and letter-writers.

(iii) *Demonstrative* or (to use the Greek term) *epideictic rhetoric* arose out of public ceremonies and rituals, where its principal duty was the praise of gods and men. Soon it embraced other forms of panegyric, such as congratulatory addresses and funeral orations. Just as each of the preceding categories can be subdivided – persuasion and dissuasion, prosecution and defence – so this came to include speeches in censure or denunciation (*vituperatio*) of an individual or institution. In all speeches of praise or condemnation the listener's attitudes and feelings may well be altered, but he is not being ostensibly persuaded to act or to reach a decision. Demonstrative oratory was still further extended to take in the sort of virtuoso exhibition, so distasteful to Socrates, at which the audience is simply a spectator or critic of the orator's skill.

THE EDUCATION OF THE ORATOR

The good orator must be a born orator, with a natural genius for his art. He will attain mastery by the study of theory, by assiduous practice in the courtroom or forum, and through the habit of imitation. The imitation of good models, always an important part of rhetorical training, came in the sixteenth century to occupy a central position in humanist education. In actual fact it must some-times have resulted in a lazy echoing of formulas and mannerisms; ideally however, it meant the assimilation of the wisdom and the virtues, as well as the literary graces, of the chosen models. One learnt through keeping the company of the great classics, just as one learnt by personal contact with the teacher, a man of culture and experience, not simply an instructor. Thomas Wilson states the theoretical position very firmly:

> Now, before we use either to write, or speake eloquently, wee must dedicate our myndes wholy, to followe the most wise and learned men, and seeke to fashion as wel their speache and gesturing, as their witte or endyting [i.e. literary compositions]. The which when we earnestly

mynd to doe, we can not but in time appere somewhat like them . . .
according to the Proverbe, by companying with the wise, a man shall
learne wisedome.

(Rhetorique, p. 5)

It is a conception which has not yet quite vanished from the
educational scene.

THE FIVE FACULTIES

The orator's training will be directed to acquiring certain skills or
faculties which together comprise the whole art of rhetoric. Cicero
provides a convenient summary of the process of rhetorical composition: the orator 'must first hit upon what to say; then manage
and marshal his discoveries, not merely in orderly fashion, but
with a discriminating eye for the exact weight . . . of each argument; next go on to array them in the adornments of style; after
that keep them guarded in his memory; and in the end deliver
them with effect and charm' (De Oratore, I. 142). The skills, in
their logical order, are invention (inventio), arrangement or disposition (τάξις, dispositio), style (λέξις, elocutio), memory, and
delivery. Under these five heads the rules of rhetoric can be drawn
up.

INVENTION is the finding or discovering of material pertinent
to the cause. It has three main branches: proof, topics, and
commonplaces. Proof, according to Aristotle, is of two kinds: the
inartificial, which is principally the evidence of the law court (for
example, sworn testimony), and the artificial or artistic, that which
is worked out by the speaker himself, using his own art and
'invention'. Artificial proof can in turn be of three kinds. (It will
by now be apparent that rhetoricians have always delighted in
classifying and subdividing.) These are:

(1) Ethos, or proof deriving from the character, especially the
moral character, of the speaker himself. Quintilian, as we have

seen, placed the highest value on evidence of the orator's virtue; for Aristotle it 'constitutes the most effective means of proof'. 'The orator,' he says, 'persuades by moral character when his speech is delivered in such a manner as to render him worthy of confidence; for we feel confidence in a greater degree and more readily in persons of worth . . .' (*Rhetoric*, I. ii. 4). Aristotle emphasizes that such 'proof' must be established within the speech itself – that is, the speaker must not rely on his public image or private reputation to do his work for him. As Quintilian saw, every aspect of the speech can reveal character: its tone will suggest the orator's good will towards his audience, and his moral concern; the ordering of his arguments will manifest his intelligence and sense of values, while the feelings which animate him will declare the goodness of his heart. This form of proof is often required in deliberative oratory and in related literary forms, as when a satirist offers an apologia for his life and writings and persuades us to endorse his right to go on vexing and mending the world.

(ii) *Pathos,* by which is usually meant the emotions induced in the audience, their favourable reactions to the orator's words. The audience begins to *feel* that the speaker must be right, and is won over to his side. The skilful rhetorician will put the hearers into a receptive frame of mind and then proceed to play upon their feelings, arousing delight or sorrow, love or hatred, indignation or mirth. It follows that the orator must understand the complexities of the human heart in order to gauge the probable responses of his audience, and to work successfully on their attitudes and foibles. To assist him, Aristotle gives an extended description of the characteristics of different age-groups. For example, the young are likely to be impulsive, full of hope, high-minded, and companion-able. They do not attach much importance to money, and 'they are fond of laughter, and therefore witty; for wit is cultured insolence' (*Rhetoric*, II. xii. 16). Conversely, the old are hesitant, small-minded, suspicious. The orator facing an audience made up predominantly of one or other of these age-groups will shape his speech accordingly. Following Aristotle's lead, the study of men's emotional dispositions became an essential part of rhetorical training. Rhetorical theory was consequently accepted as an authoritative source of information about the passions, 'until Descartes proposed a "scientific" treatment of them different only in details' (Richard McKeon, 'Rhetoric in the Middle Ages', *Speculum*, XVII (1942), p. 32).

(iii) *Logical Proof*, or demonstration of the case by means of argument, may necessitate the use of syllogisms and other strictly logical procedures. More characteristically the orator will deploy the *enthymeme*, the example (*exemplum*) and the maxim (*sententia*). Illustrative *exempla* may be taken from history or fable; the story of the belly which Menenius relates for the benefit of the Roman citizenry in the opening scene of *Coriolanus* is an obvious instance. The *maxim* is simply the kind of general statement or truth which commands immediate assent. The plays of Euripides are thickly sown with them and Aristotle has no difficulty in culling several specimens: 'No man who is sensible ought to have his children taught to be excessively clever';[1] 'There is no man who is happy in everything.' Dryden, at the other end of the rhetorical tradition, is also fond of this persuasive device: 'For no man's Faith depends upon his Will'; 'Short is the date of all immoderate Fame'. The maxim, as in these examples, will often have the further value of expressing the speaker's *ethos*, since it plainly declares his 'moral preferences' (Aristotle, *Rhetoric*, II. xxi. 16).

The remaining subdivisions of Invention are the *topics* and the *commonplaces*. The topics (τόποι, literally 'places,' or more specifically places where stores and treasure are kept) are tested and approved ways of investigating a chosen subject, ways both of conducting an argument and of analysing a theme or subject prior to discussing it. Aristotle sets out twenty-eight topics of argument,

[1] Aristotle also uses this maxim as the premise of an enthymeme: see p. 14 above.

such as the *a fortiori* ('if a man beats his father he will also beat his neighbours'). From this store the speaker may select arguments best fitted to his case. Similarly in the treatment of a theme. If, for example, a speaker is preparing a panegyric on a particular individual he will begin by asking himself: On what grounds, in general, are men accorded praise? By answering his question systematically (and with the aid of the text-books) he can compile a catalogue of the topics of praise and relate each item to the matter in hand. He may decide that praise can be fittingly derived from the topic of ancestry; from his subject's services to his country; even from his place of birth: 'The Shire or Towne helpeth somewhat, towardes the encrease of honor: As it is much better to bee borne in Paris, then in Picardie: in London then in Lincolne. For that both the ayre is better, the people more civill, and the wealth much greater, and the men for the most part more wise' (Wilson, *Rhetorique*, p. 13). The *topics*, properly used, are aids to composition, well-tried methods of stimulating thought, and safeguards against the haphazard selection of ideas. They help to ensure that the subject is thoroughly covered. Their disadvantage is that they can become substitutes for real thought, recipes from which laborious and stiff speeches are prepared. Blair dismisses them curtly: 'Where Cicero has had recourse to them, his Orations are so much the worse on that account' (*Lectures*, vol. II, p. 182).

In the early rhetorics, *commonplaces* (κοινοὶ τόποι) are those topics of argument which are common to different subject areas. In this sense it is a commonplace that we cannot judge the merits of an action until we have scrutinized the motives of the agent — for this argument may be utilized in many oratorical situations, in a demonstrative panegyric, a speech for the prosecution, or a political persuasion. Later the name was applied to any observation or truth which is pithily expressed, weighty and serviceable: time flies; death is common to all. Commonplaces like these are similar to the maxim in form and effect. Others are simply general topics (in the non-rhetorical sense), matters of perennial interest which might be proposed as subjects for debate or taken as themes for oratorical or poetic variations: the mutability of things; the contemplative versus the active life. One reason why the noble commonplaces of rhetoric have shrunk into the triteness of the modern 'commonplace' is illustrated by the speeches of Justice Shallow: 'Certain, 'tis certain; very sure, very sure: death, as the Psalmist saith, is certain to all; all shall die. How a good yoke of bullocks at Stamford fair?'

The second of the orator's skills, ARRANGEMENT, fashions both the disposition of his arguments and the structure of his speech. The number of parts into which a speech is divided will depend on its nature and circumstances, and on the teachings of the theorists. Aristotle thinks there are really only two: statement of the case and proof, to which an *exordium* and *epilogue* may be added. Thomas Wilson begins by enumerating seven subdivisions, but at once makes an exception for encomiastic orations, where proof is irrelevant. At its fullest, when used in legal cases, the classical oration will contain the following sections, usually in the following order:

(1) The *exordium*, or *prooemium*, or *proem*, or *introduction*. Its all-important function is to put the hearer into the right frame of mind, to make him, according to the often repeated formula, 'well-disposed, attentive, and receptive' ('benivolum, attentum, docilem'; Cicero, *De Inventione*, I. 20). Attention must be aroused, perhaps by a promise of important things to follow. The speaker will secure the favour of the audience by describing his own character and conduct, by flattering the judges, or by drawing the hearers into a personal relationship with him: 'Friends, Romans, countrymen. . . .' These are the tactics of the *direct* opening. The subtler approach of the indirect exordium (what Cicero calls *insinuatio*) is required if the orator has to overcome any resistance in his audience, or if the nature of his case puts him at a disadvantage. He

may then choose to begin with a fable, an anecdote, or a jest, perhaps fastening on some expression in his adversary's speech and turning it to ridicule.

(2) The *narration* or narrative (*narratio*); a short statement of the facts of the case. In a judicial oration it is essential that this be clear and cogent.

(3) *Proposition* or exposition, in which the orator either states succinctly the concern of his speech, or sets a definite issue or problem before the audience. At this point he will if necessary define his terms, as recommended by Socrates.

(4) *Division* (*partitio*, sometimes also called *divisio*), which is frequently combined with the *proposition*. The speaker shows how he proposes to treat the subject under certain main heads. It was agreed that too many headings would only confuse an audience, and three was settled upon as the optimum number (*Ad Herennium*, I. x. 17). A carefully formulated *division* promises a carefully organized discourse to follow. It helps the speaker to hold the principal points in his mind and makes recapitulation easier; it affords the hearer a preliminary view of the whole, enabling him to keep track of the speaker's progress. Brian Vickers has shown how for many Renaissance authors, including Hooker, Sidney, Burton and Bacon, *partitio* was still a vital organizing principle (*Francis Bacon*, ch. 2). By the eighteenth century it was not commonly found outside the sermon.

(5) *Proof*, or confirmation (*confirmatio*), in which the orator marshals all the arguments on his side of the case, is the core of the speech. Classical authorities usually advocated that the arguments be set out in a military formation, strong ones coming first, the weakest sheltered in the centre, and the most powerful bringing up the rear. By the time of Blair we are recommended to 'advance in the way of climax', disposing our points in an ascending order of importance (*Lectures*, vol. II, p. 185). It is advice which has been given to generations of essay-writers.

The judicial bias of classical rhetoric is clearly seen in the central place given to *proof*, which in a demonstrative speech may often be dispensed with. We find that either the definition of *confirmatio* (though not its name) is modified to take in, say, the substance of a panegyric; or that such material is accommodated elsewhere, usually in the *narratio*.

(6) *Refutation* (*refutatio* or *reprehensio*); here the orator attempts to answer or discredit the arguments which are likely to be, or have already been, advanced against him.

(7) *Conclusion* or peroration, normally containing the following subsections:

(a) a summing up (*enumeratio*) of the main points.

(b) amplification (*amplificatio*, also called *indignatio*), an impressive affirmation or emphatic statement of the speaker's position. He will use *commonplaces* to move the audience to indignation or enthusiasm. In a judicial speech he will dwell on the foulness of the crime, 'accompanying the narration with reproaches and violent denunciations of each act, and by [his] language bring[ing] the action as vividly as possible before the eyes of the judge . . .' (*De Inventione*, I. 104).

(c) an appeal to the tender feelings of the audience (*conquestio* or *commiseratio*). Commonplaces such as 'the vicissitudes of fortune' help to arouse pity and subdue hostile passions. Or the speaker may lament his ill-luck, while going on to show that he will be brave and patient in adversity. Cicero sensibly remarks that it is advisable not to linger over the *conquestio*, 'for a tear is quickly dried, especially when shed for the misfortunes of others' (*De Partitione Oratoria*, 57). Paradoxically, a *conclusion* may appear during the course of a speech: the orator may make use of amplification or *conquestio* to underline one of his strongest arguments, and he may sum up his discussion at the end of each important stage.

This elaborate structural scheme was the outcome of much theorising and much practical experience. It survived because it seemed to offer helpful and effective ways of organizing material, helpful not only to the politician and the homilist, but also to Sidney, preparing a defence of poetry, and to Pope, preparing a defence of his own poetry in the *Epistle to Dr Arbuthnot*. It lingers on, much emaciated, in rules and hints for writing essays and other forms of expository prose. Blair, for instance, gives some advice to the preacher which is still considered relevant to the schoolboy: if we use the *conclusion* to draw inferences from what we have previously said, then we must beware of introducing some entirely new and distracting point (*Lectures*, vol. II, p. 200). It is advice which deserves to be repeated because it is soundly practical.

Three faculties of the orator remain to be discussed: style, memory and delivery. Of these the two last, which can be more briefly dealt with, may be taken first.

MEMORY. Classical rhetoricians agree that although a speech is a product of reflection and art it ought to seem unpremeditated, and should whenever possible be delivered from memory. The rhetorical manuals normally give some guidance on memory-training, the oldest extant treatment being that in the *Ad Herennium*, whose author recommends a visual mnemonic system whereby symbolic objects and figures are placed in sharply visualized 'backgrounds' or scenes.

For the spoken oration DELIVERY (*pronuntiatio*) is all-important. Without effective delivery the speech loses its impact, whether it be a sermon, a lawyer's plea, a political harangue, or a lecture. '*Demosthenes* therefore, that famous Oratour, beeing asked what was the chiefest point in all Oratorie, gave the chiefe and onely praise to Pronunciation; being demaunded, what was the second, and the third, he stil made aunswere Pronunciation, and would make no other aunswere till they left asking, declaring hereby, that arte without utteraunce can doe nothing, utteraunce without art can doe right much' (Wilson, *Rhetorique*, p. 218; the story is related in Cicero's *Brutus*, 142). The orator must use the appropriate gestures ('suit the action to the word, the word to the action') and facial expression. He must master the standard repertory of the public speaker – the wagging finger of exhortation, the arms and hands spread in appeal. The orator is here close kin to the actor (in Greek, rhetorical delivery and the art of acting are both called ὑπόκρισις) and Bertram Joseph has argued that the style of acting which prevailed in the Elizabethan theatre was based on a codified system of gestures derived from oratory.

Like the actor the public speaker must study voice control. The *Ad Herennium* (III. xiii–xiv) describes three tones of voice, advising the orator to be guided in his choice by the over-riding principle of decorum:

(i) the conversational tone, which is relaxed and close to the manner of ordinary speech (*sermo*). It has a wide range, from the dignified and serious to the facetious.

(ii) the tone of debate (*contentio*), which is characterized by energy; it may be 'sustained' or 'broken' and exclamatory.

(iii) that of amplification, suitable for the conclusion of a speech. In order to evoke pity the voice will be restrained, the tone deep and full, the pauses long.

It seems probable that the rhetorical theory of tone directly influenced the style of works which were written to be read aloud, or which deliberately tried to suggest the accents of the speaking voice. In such cases an author would seek linguistic and stylistic equivalents for the various tones, as Geoffrey Shepherd has suggested in the case of the *Ancrene Wisse*. Horace certainly developed a tone close to that of conversation for his satires and epistles, poems which he referred to as *sermones*.

STYLE. Aristotle begins by distinguishing two kinds of prose style, one appropriate to debate and the other, more precise and controlled, suitable for 'written compositions', by which he seems primarily to mean demonstrative orations. The style of debate he then further breaks down into an 'ethical' manner for legal pleading and an 'emotional' one for deliberative speeches (*Rhetoric*, III. xii. 1–2). This gives a three-fold division corresponding to the three kinds of oratory; yet it is a division based on two pairs of contrasted terms: debating and written, ethical and emotional. A contrast between two kinds of style is also found in Cicero, who in the main adheres to the three-fold scheme: 'there are two distinct types of good oratory ... one simple and concise, the other elevated and abundant' (*Brutus*, 201). Underlying this contrast of styles is a contrast between two different uses of language, as a means of communication and as a vehicle of feeling and imagination – a contrast which has had a long history. De Quincey reformulated it in terms of 'literature of knowledge' and 'literature of power', and I. A. Richards as a distinction between 'scientific' and 'emotive' language (*Principles of Literary Criticism*, 3rd ed., New York and London, 1928, ch. 34).

Meanwhile, the classification of style according to the three types of oratory seems to have been evolved by Theophrastus, in a work now lost, and then adopted by Cicero and later writers:

(i) The grand style (*genus grande* or *grave*) is composed of impressive words, ornately arranged. This is an art-ful style, well suited to the conclusion of a speech, able to move and persuade the audience.

(ii) The middle style is more relaxed, and less elevated in diction, though never stooping to the colloquial. It is essentially pleasurable.

(iii) The low, or plain, or simple style (*genus humile* or *extenuatum*) uses current speech idiom and a conversational manner; it is suitable for proof and instruction.

Orators are advised to master all three kinds, and to avoid the faulty styles which are their close neighbours. The grand style, inexpertly handled, becomes swollen and blustering, the diction more impressive than the theme demands. (We may observe that the teachers of rhetoric constantly stand on guard against the very same bombastic turgidities that 'rhetoric' has come to denote.) Likewise, the middle style can degenerate into a slack, diffuse way of writing that fails to grasp and enunciate the ideas it is trying to present. The simple style may sink into meagreness and unvaried triviality.

In addition there are qualities of style which are common to all three categories and indeed essential to them all. These, too, were probably first classified by Theophrastus and subsequently developed by Cicero in his *De Oratore*:

(1) *purity* and correctness of language. Good usage should be our standard, and we must avoid all barbarisms and solecisms.

(2) *clarity* and intelligibility.

(3) *decorum*, or the quality of appropriateness, a quality not simply of style alone, but of every aspect of a formal oration. Art is here at one with Nature. In conversation we adapt what we are saying, our tone of voice, and our gestures, to fit the occasion and the person we are addressing. A facetious manner would be tactless at a solemn gathering. Cicero's faith in decorum was absolute: 'in omni parte orationis ut vitae quid deceat est considerandum' ('the universal rule, in oratory as in life, is to consider propriety': *Orator*, 71). Quintilian, who treats the subject in even greater detail, predictably adds a moral dimension: it is proper for 'all men at all times and in all places . . . to act and speak as befits a man of honour' (XI. i. 14). Virtue is always appropriate.

(4) *ornament*, or the decorative aspects of style, especially figures of speech and prose rhythm. The *figures* or *schemes* (*figurae*, σχήματα) are literally 'attitudes', the different postures taken up by words on different occasions. Like human postures they are expressive of meaning. Gorgias was credited with being

their 'inventor', or more precisely the first to introduce an orna-
mental style into prose from poetry, where metaphor, alliteration
and other devices were already well established. Their ultimate
origins are probably to be sought in the language of primitive
religions and magic. Periphrasis and metonymy enable men to
refer to divinities without risking the disaster that might ensue if
the sacred names themselves were to be uttered (Curtius, *European
Literature*, p. 275).

As the theory and practice of rhetoric developed, increasing
attention was paid to ornament. The Greeks seem to have derived
considerable aesthetic pleasure from 'artistically elaborated discourse' and the musical possibilities of words (Curtius, pp. 64 and
388). The Renaissance delight in recognizing the figures is revealed
in a well-known comment by 'E.K.' on two lines in Spenser's
Shepheardes Calender:

> I love thilke lasse, (alas why doe I love?)
> And am forlorne, (alas why am I lorne?)
>
> ('January', 61–2)

A modern reader does not require a knowledge of rhetoric in order
to hear how each parenthesis plaintively echoes what has gone
before. 'E.K.', however, says nothing about the mood of the lines
(perhaps he takes it as read), but concentrates on their craftsman-
ship: 'a prety Epanorthosis [a retracting or correcting of what has
just been said] in these two verses, and withall a Paranomasia or
playing with the word [lasse/alas].' We get the impression that the
process of naming the ornaments was something to be enjoyed in
its own right.

The treatises continued to refine upon the figures, and to
increase the already abundant store. The *Ad Herennium* lists
sixty-five; the first edition of Henry Peacham's *Garden of Eloquence* (1577) contains nearly two hundred. Enjoyment was also
evidently derived from the subtle task of discriminating between

ornaments which are similar in form. Take the matter of questions. These, as Quintilian remarks, 'admit of infinite variety'. We are taught by the rhetorical textbooks to distinguish between:

interrogatio: a question which requires no answer, because it expresses a truth which cannot be denied. So Quintilian, speaking of decorum, asks 'Can sorrow be expressed in epigram?' (XI. i. 52). This is a powerful device, beloved of all orators, since it implies and exploits agreement between the speaker and his audience. Hence, though it does not ask for assent it often receives a distinctly audible response. It has come to be known, significantly, as a 'rhetorical question'.

rogatio: a question to which we immediately supply our own answer, as in Falstaff's 'Counterfeit? I lie, I am no counterfeit.'

quaesitio: a string of questions uttered in rapid succession for the sake of emotional emphasis.

percontatio: an enquiry addressed to another person (or to oneself) in a tone of bewilderment or amazement, and allowing of no satisfactory or easy reply. As when Sir Thomas Bertram's return disrupts the theatricals at Mansfield Park: 'How is the consternation of the party to be described?' Or we may put our question in a spirit of reproach and upbraiding. The classic example is the opening of Cicero's speech against Catiline, which combines *percontatio* with *quaesitio*, and illustrates, in its second sentence, how *percontatio* shades into *exclamatio*: 'In the name of heaven, Catilina, how long will you exploit our patience? Surely your insane activities cannot escape our retaliation for ever! Are there to be no limits to this swaggering, ungovernable recklessness?' (*Selected Political Speeches*, p. 76).

One of the consequences of this fascination with the figures is that ornament, originally only one among four qualities of style, assumed a dominant position in rhetoric as a whole. Another was that rhetoricians, being habitually tidy and systematic, attempted to reduce the multifarious ornaments to some kind of order. It was customary in Hellenistic rhetoric to divide *figures of words* from *figures of thought*. To clarify a distinction that was by no means always clear to the rhetoricians themselves, Quintilian quotes a sentence from Cicero's Verrine Orations: 'Iam iam, Dolabella, neque me tui neque tuorum liberum' ('Now, Dolabella, [I have no pity] either for you or for your children': Second Speech against Verres, I. xxx. 77). The *figure of thought* consists in Cicero's turning from the judges, to whom he has been narrating past events, in order to make a direct address to the absent Dolabella, who had joined Verres in crime and been double-crossed. Once Cicero had conceived this move he could have carried it out in a variety of ways. As it is, he has chosen to give sharp definition to the figure of thought by using two *figures of words*: a reduplication (*iam iam*) and the contracted form *liberum* (Quintilian, IX. i. 16).

A further category and complication is introduced by designating some figures of words as *tropes*, leaving the terms *figure* and *scheme* to cover the remainder. The theorists would argue that in the example above the word *iam* has its ordinary prose meaning; it is the repetition of the word which creates the artistic figure. In a figure or scheme, as distinct from a trope, the sense of each individual word remains the same as in ordinary speech, though the form into which the words are cast does not. On the other hand, when a word is invented for expressive effect (onomatopoeia), or used in a sense other than its 'normal' one (metaphor, metonymy, etc.), or with a covert, secret meaning (irony, allegory) we have a *trope* (literally a 'turn'), defined by Quintilian as 'the artistic alteration of a word or phrase from its proper meaning to another' (VIII. vi. 1). This distinction was carefully preserved. It is for example adhered to in Bede's *De Schematibus et Tropis*, written in the early eighth century as a textbook for the monastic school at Jarrow; in the mid-sixteenth century Richard Sherry published a *Treatise of Schemes and Tropes*.

As tropes seemed more audacious and more powerfully emotive than the figures they were bound to receive rather fuller attention, especially since Aristotle had exalted metaphor as a mark of genius, and Quintilian had called it the supreme ornament of poetry. But the schemes were not neglected. Chief among them were the so-called 'Gorgianic figures', which passed through the medium of Latin medieval prose to re-emerge in the intense stylizations of Lyly. Two of these figures may be illustrated here:

Isocolon, the use of clauses or phrases of equal length. (A *colon* is originally either a clause or, more often, a brief and grammatically complete sentence which yet does not fully express the speaker's meaning and is therefore combined with other *cola* to form a *period*.) Examples of *isocolon* are frequently found in antitheses, where the verbal figure reinforces the balance or contrast of the idea expressed. In such cases form and thought work so harmoniously together as to throw the neat rhetorical classifications into disarray. The ingenuity of the traditional rhetoricians was sorely tried by the figure *antithesis*, which was sometimes placed with the figures of thought, sometimes with those of words, sometimes with both. Worse still, some kinds of antithesis make the 'change from normal meaning' criterion, used to differentiate tropes from figures, look rather wooden and inadequate. Here is an example from Farquhar's *Beaux' Stratagem*: 'Fortune has taken the weak under her protection, but men of sense are left to their industry' (Act I). The balanced form (the two *cola* of roughly equal length) encourages us to think of 'the weak' and 'men of sense' as decidedly contrasted with one another. The formal framework brings both terms to a sharp focus of opposition so that each helps to define the meaning of the other. One characteristic of 'the weak' would appear to be their lack of good sense. More important, the 'men of sense' (and it is one of their representatives who is speaking) are by implication strong and courageous. The figure *isocolon* is part of the context in which the words operate, and as such it affects their meanings. In rhetorical terms, this scheme has something of the trope about it.

Parison: a parallelism of form (grammatical and syntactical structure) between two or more *cola* – as in the second line of this couplet from Pope's *Essay on Man*:

> Is it for thee the lark ascends and sings?
> Joy tunes his voice, joy elevates his wings.
>
> (Epistle III, 31–2)

Parison is here strengthened by *anaphora* (repetition of a word at the beginning of consecutive clauses or sentences). The result is a firm repudiation of the proud and selfish assumption that nature exists for man. The formal symmetry effects this repudiation without the poet having to fall back on a simple negative, which might seem to be taking the absurd question of the first line too solemnly. So the rhetoric is a sign of Pope's absolute control over his argument and his feelings.

Some patterns of words are also patterns of movement or rhythm, as Cicero remarked: 'If [words] have similar case-endings [the figure *homoioteleuton*], or if clauses are equally balanced, or if contrary ideas are opposed, the sentence becomes rhythmical by its very nature, even if no rhythm is intended' (*Orator*, 164). This kind of symmetrical movement was first developed by Gorgias and Thrasymachus of Chalcedon. To Cicero it seemed mannered and affected. He preferred 'the well-knit rhythm of prose' (*Orator*, 168), which appears unstudied, the natural expression of thought and emotion. 'Every passage which does not halt or waver, but advances steadily and uniformly is considered rhythmical' (*Orator*, 198). His ideal of full and rounded periods is one with his ideal of *copia*, that fullness and adequacy of style which takes a middle way between brevity and diffuseness, and which suggests strength of mind, magnanimity and conscious rectitude.

Something remains to be said about the *figures of thought*, which as I have indicated, are more inclusive in scope than those of words. Among them we find catalogued what we now think of as major features of literary works. Such is the *character-sketch*, which the orator may employ when praising or discrediting an individual, and when arousing pity or indignation. Collections of such characters, illustrating the varieties of human nature and conduct, were established as a minor literary genre by Theophrastus. Or the figure of thought may control in a general way the presentation of material, as in the case of *descriptio*. Here the orator paints in lively colours the probable consequences of some action or event, the stock example being the prophetic description of the aftermath of a successful siege. Related to *descriptio*, and sometimes confused with it, is *demonstratio* (ἐνάργεια), the vivid and detailed recounting of an actual event so as to bring it sharply before the eyes of the audience. Cicero, as we have seen, recommends this technique for the conclusion of a speech. It is the method used by Burke in narrating the attack on Versailles (*Reflections on the Revolution in France*, ed. Conor Cruise O'Brien, Harmondsworth, 1969, pp. 164–5). We have here an anticipation of the celebrated contrast between the artist who tells and the artist who shows, for Quintilian writes of the difference between merely narrating facts and displaying them in their living truth to the eyes of the mind (VIII. iii. 62).

Since *enargeia* is a dramatic technique, appropriate to describe actions, it became entangled with the similar concept of *energeia*, or vigour, activity, and purposeful movement, a concept which in Aristotle passes easily into the idea of actuality. Aristotle saw *energeia* at its most memorable in Homer, who 'gives movement and life' to everything and so gives everything actuality, for 'actuality is movement' (*Rhetoric*, III. xi. 2–4). What these confusions of terminology point to is the recognition that vividness and dramatic immediacy are essential for all the orator's most demanding tasks, and that the figures can best generate this necessary 'energy'. We find Longinus saying that the word *image* is currently applied 'to passages in which, carried away by your feelings, you imagine you are actually seeing the subject of your description, and enable your audience as well to see it' (*On the Sublime*, trans. T. S. Dorsch, p. 121). The continuity of the rhetorical tradition emerges in Dryden's definition of the 'proper wit' of a heroic or historical poem: 'some lively and apt description, dressed in such colours of speech that it sets before your eyes the absent object as perfectly and more delightfully than nature' (Preface to *Annus Mirabilis*, in *Of Dramatic Poesy and other Critical Essays*, ed. George Watson, London, 1962, vol. I, p. 98). As a result of this way of thinking, imagery has sometimes been considered exclusively a matter of *visual* images.

There is always a danger that the weaker artist may succumb to the fatal fascination of patterns and schemes and produce merely elaborate concoctions. The teachers of rhetoric, aware of this possibility, continually urge that figures must be used with caution and moderation. Cicero reminds us of their serious and expressive function: 'They are not so important in heightening the colour of words, as in throwing ideas into a stronger light' (*Brutus*, 141). The figures enforce meaning, as in the examples I have quoted from Pope and Farquhar. So it is in ordinary life, where the need to express urgency or irritation or determination leads us to repeat words and phrases. Vindice's 'Nine coaches waiting – hurry, hurry, hurry' (Tourneur, *The Revenger's Tragedy*, II. i) is only a slight exaggeration of a common enough tendency in speech. 'So like, as a rule, is nature to art' (Quintilian, VIII. iii. 86). This dictum occurs when Quintilian is discussing emphatic statements, for which we regularly call on the figures to assist us. But if nature and art are alike they are not identical, a belief which leads him into some difficulty. When he comes to examine the figure of exclamation he goes so far as to say that when exclamations 'are genuine [*vera*] they do not come under the head of [figures]: it is only those which are simulated and artfully designed [*simulata et arte composita*] which can with any certainty be regarded as figures' (IX. ii. 27). This raises more problems than it solves. How can we be certain that the orator is in earnest? At what point does exaggeration turn into simulation? The bogeys of 'intention' and 'sincerity' are not far away. It seems almost as if Quintilian's hand is poised to open the floodgates of that violent reaction against rhetoric which would set the genuine and sincere against all that is feigned and counterfeit. The difficulty is that any honest rhetorician must acknowledge the natural basis of the figures, but that Nature, once admitted to the discussion, raises very disturbing questions. One reason for the downfall of the whole rhetorical structure at the end of the eighteenth century was the realization that the use of even the boldest figures is a characteristic of great poets and orators, primitive societies, and common people alike: 'there is nowhere more use made of figures than in the lowest and most vulgar conversation' (Adam Smith, *Lectures on Rhetoric*, p. 30). This in turn has led to the perception that metaphor is a basic mental process, a way of coming to grips with the world, 'the omnipresent principle of language' (I. A. Richards, *Philosophy of Rhetoric*, p. 92). The nature of figurative language has had to be thought out afresh.

That the rhetorical framework survived so long, in spite of such local inconsistencies and uncertainties as we have noted in Quintilian, is partly owing to the fact that later rhetoricians placed Art firmly at the centre of their considerations, and kept Nature away on the circumference. In the Renaissance there was what may seem in retrospect a rather anxious over-stressing of the fact that schemes and tropes are divergences from the norm of language, something 'much unlike to that which men commonly use to speake' (Wilson, *Rhetorique*, p. 170). Puttenham calls them 'in a sorte abuses or rather trespasses in speach', and 'transgressions of our dayly speach' (*Arte of English Poesie*, pp. 154, 262). Yet at the very end of his discussion Nature is admitted: 'all your figures Poeticall or Rhetoricall, are but observations of strange speeches, and such as without any arte at al we should use, and commonly do, even by very nature without discipline.' Puttenham is clearly thinking out his position as he goes along. The final result is difficult to reconcile with his earlier statements, but it represents a satisfactory working compromise, a return to the basic classical tenet that art and nature must co-operate: 'so as we may conclude, that nature her selfe suggesteth the figure in this or that forme: but arte aydeth the judgement of his [i.e. its] use and application' (p. 298).

This last stage of Puttenham's argument could be illustrated by the case of *hyperbole*, the figure which he engagingly re-christens 'the over-reacher or the loud liar.' It is a device that is put to daily use in emphatic assertions, denials, and boasts. 'Nature her selfe suggesteth the figure.' But in the hands of the skilful persuader a hyperbole is not simply a means of drumming up feelings or exaggerating the enormity of an action. It may also serve to focus attitudes which have been growing throughout a whole discourse, as in Burke's indignant protest over the fate of Marie Antoinette: 'I thought ten thousand swords must have leaped from their scabbards to avenge even a look that threatened her with insult' (*Reflections*, p. 170). James Boulton points out that this exaggeration 'gives heightened expression ... to that notion of the instinctive defence of womanhood which is the traditional proof of humane feelings'. The overthrow of order in revolutionary France means the collapse of standards of behaviour and the downfall of magnanimity. For Burke the mob's treatment of the Queen marks the ultimate degradation of the French people. In order to intensify our sense of that degradation he exaggerates the chivalric impulse to protect the weak, the very opposite of the mob's barbarity. That noble impulse is now dead: 'But the age of chivalry is gone. – That of sophisters, oeconomists, and calculators, has succeeded; and the glory of Europe is extinguished for ever' (*Reflections*, p. 170; Boulton, *The Language of Politics*, p. 132). Properly used, the figures are never merely decorative, but powerfully expressive and moving. 'There is no more effective method of exciting the emotions,' says Quintilian, 'than an apt use of figures' (IX. i. 21).

4
Rhetoric and Literature

RHETORIC IN EDUCATION

The very considerable impact of rhetoric on literature was a consequence of its central place in classical, medieval and Renaissance education. Paradoxically, it was the decline of public oratory in Rome that gave a new impetus to the study of rhetoric. After the fall of the Republic occasions for deliberative oratory decreased, while forensic oratory became increasingly specialized. The energies of the theorists were directed into educational channels, and in the schools of rhetoric the subject was studied intensely and with ultimately fruitful results. The pupils analysed and composed orations of various kinds. They would also declaim speeches in the guise of some other person, a hero or legendary character (the figure of thought known as *prosopopoeia*). This is an imaginative extension of the quite common practice among rhetoricians of writing speeches for clients to deliver. And it is acknowledged by Quintilian to be a valuable exercise for future poets and historians (III. viii. 49), encouraging sympathy and understanding, developing that 'awareness' of other people which T. S. Eliot has claimed as an essential quality in the dramatist. Already the techniques of rhetoric are helping to develop excellence in other fields.

In the school curriculum of the Middle Ages rhetoric, grammar, and dialectic (or logic) composed the *trivium* – literally 'three roads' – the first group of subjects to be mastered. Together with the *quadrivium* (arithmetic, geometry, music, astronomy) these made up the seven Liberal Arts. Poetry was assigned sometimes to the care of grammar, sometimes to rhetoric. The subjects of the *trivium* are of fundamental importance because they are all, including logic, arts of communication. This view derives from an analogy made by Zeno the Stoic, and related by Cicero: 'clenching his fist he said logic was like that; relaxing and extending his hand, he said eloquence was like the open palm' (*Orator*, 113). Logic is the tighter, more austere method of communicating ideas to the learned world; it is the discourse of philosophers, whereas eloquence is the open, expressive discourse of the orator and popularizer: 'Eloquence is nothing else but wisdom delivering copious utterance' (Cicero, *De Partitione Oratoria*, 79).

The work of Rodolphus Agricola (d. 1485) marks a change of course. For him, as for Socrates, the prime function of logic was not to communicate the truth but to enquire after it. Dialectic has a monopoly in the search for wisdom, and rhetoric is restricted to methods of presentation. Agricola's achievement was overshadowed by the more thorough-going educational reforms carried out by Petrus Ramus (Pierre de la Ramée, 1515–1572). Irritated by the muddles and duplications of the existing curriculum, Ramus was impelled to reorganize. Vagueness and confusion were anathema to his unremittingly practical mind. He therefore redefined the roles of logic and rhetoric, arguing that in its handling of Invention and Arrangement rhetoric was repeating work that was already, and better, done by the logicians in their treatment of *inventio* and *judicium* (judgment). Stripped of these, rhetoric is left with style and delivery. Ramus is concerned not to depreciate rhetoric but only to redistribute material more tidily. The man who writes and delivers a speech is, so to speak, two men; he is a logician when he prepares and disposes his subject matter, and a rhetorician only when he presents his material to his audience. In Ramus' view, every great work of literature, like every effective speech, endures because it has its basis in dialectic, because it is an expression of man's search for truth, and is susceptible to logical analysis. Ramus' educational programme therefore insisted on the reading of the poets and orators, and drew special attention to the logical aspects of literature. His textbook of the reformed logic, *Dialecticae Libri Duo*, exemplifies points with illustrations from the poets. According to Rosemond Tuve it tends towards making a 'virtual identification of poetry with dialectic' (*Elizabethan and Metaphysical Imagery*, p. 334).

In sixteenth-century England, Ramist doctrines were popular at Cambridge, where they may have influenced Spenser, Greene, and Sidney, and where they certainly influenced Gabriel Harvey. It seems to have been Harvey who introduced into English education the Ramist idea (itself only a codification of traditional practice) that rhetorical training should consist of two parts: a process of *analysis*, or critical reading, followed by *genesis*, the complementary process of composition. *Analysis* is concerned with the close examination of texts, the study of the ways in which authors achieve their effects, the recognition of the figures they use. Quintilian had dwelt on the merit of this kind of classroom exercise: a boy should read out a speech, or a passage from one of the historians, with the teacher pointing out its virtues and failings and also questioning his pupils in order to develop their critical powers, encouraging them 'to find out things for themselves and to use their intelligence, which is after all the chief aim of this method of training' (II. v. 5–17). In the sixteenth century Quintilian was himself an object of such analytical attention. It was then also common practice for schoolboys to be asked to reproduce or summarize the contents of the Sunday sermon (a deliberative oration) on the following day. We can assume that such habits of careful listening were not forgotten in the playhouse.

As an aid to composition the student would prepare his own

personal anthology. Gems of wit and wisdom encountered in his reading would be entered in his 'commonplace book'. Bacon recommended the making of these compilations, provided they were the genuine product of individual reading, on the grounds that they would ensure 'copie [copiousness] of invention' and contract 'judgment to a strength' (*Advancement of Learning*). Jonson, Webster, and Chapman all drew upon their own collections when writing their plays. The student would also note down felicities of style for future use. Or he could turn to published sources, like the *Thesaurus Ciceronianus* (1535) of Marius Nizolius, who brought together all the pearls of Ciceronian expression so that the imitator could help himself. Sidney's protest against these works is made on behalf, not of originality of utterance (which might lead only to eccentricity), but of genuine imitation which is based on a thorough assimilation of the chosen model:

> Truly I could wish ... the diligent imitators of Tully and Demosthenes (most worthy to be imitated) did not so much keep Nizolian paper-books of their figures and phrases, as by attentive translation (as it were) devour them whole, and make them wholly theirs.
>
> (*Apology*, ed. Shepherd, p. 138)

Such 'attentive translation' can be truly educational, a way of growing in understanding.

Imitation, as Sidney conceived it, was the technique that governed all processes of composition. The pupil might be set to write a declamation, an exercise which was still being prescribed in grammar school and university curricula in the eighteenth century. He would also be required from time to time to compose a *chria*, a short oration developing a moral theme. By speaking in praise of fortitude, for example, or against tyranny, he would be helping to inculcate the love of good and the hatred of evil in his schoolfellows' breasts. Those leaving school to pursue further studies made their farewell in a Latin oration; at the University they would take part in disputations and debates on more abstract and complex issues.

In the habit of *analysis*, as it was advocated in the rhetorical treatises and followed out in the classroom, we can see the beginnings of later critical techniques. For *analysis*, like its more sophisticated descendant, Practical Criticism, required close reading and attention to detail. Its virtues are displayed in many of Quintilian's observations on the figures. He quotes, for instance, from one of Dido's soliloquies:

> Non licuit thalami expertem sine crimine vitam
> Degere more ferae?
>
> *(Aeneid,* IV, 550–1)

('Ah, that I could not spend my life, apart from wedlock, a blameless life, even as some wild creature. . . .') Quintilian observes that 'although Dido complains of marriage, yet her passionate outburst shows that she regards life without wedlock as no life for man, but for the beasts of the field' (IX. ii. 64). In Pope's *Essay on Criticism* Quintilian is fittingly given a place of honour among the true critics, and his doctrines are cited in Pope's own notes to the poem.

As the eighteenth century went on rhetoric increasingly occupied itself with general questions of style and form, and drew even closer to criticism. Blair still thinks of the processes of analysis (what he calls judging and relishing the beauties of a work) and composition as complementary. 'Whatever enables genius to execute well, will enable taste to criticize justly' (*Lectures,* vol. I, p. 8). But the balance is tilting towards analysis, since taste is more amenable to instruction than genius. Creative writing is for the gifted few to pursue in private; the new-style rhetorician carries out the humbler tasks of giving advice on prose composition, and educating taste. Such duties may be humble, but they are also undoubtedly moral. Because Blair holds the classical belief in the close relationship between effective discourse and the 'virtuous affections' – the good orator must be a good man – he conceives criticism as instruction in 'the philosophy of human nature', in self-knowledge and in 'disposing the heart to virtue' (vol. I. pp. 9–10, 13).

Being of central and continuing importance in education, rhetoric was bound to influence all aspects of communication, including ordinary conversation. In *The Taming of the Shrew* Tranio, playing with the traditional distinction between learned logic and popular rhetoric, advises his master to keep logic-chopping and disputation for his friends, and to 'practise rhetoric in your common talk' (I. i. 35). We can recognize the rhetorical sources of the advice that was freely given, during the seventeenth and eighteenth centuries, on politeness and conversation – advice about ordering and arranging one's conversational materials to the best advantage, about observing decorum and avoiding all pedantry and jargon. Men were encouraged to cultivate speech as a vehicle of communication, putting the needs of their hearers uppermost, rather than as a means of self-expression. 'We are prompted by the strongest motives,' says Blair, 'to study how we may communicate our thoughts to one another with most advantage.' The very strongest of these motives is precisely that sense of the sanctity of language which inspired Isocrates and which was at the root of medieval and Renaissance education:

> One of the most distinguished privileges which Providence has conferred upon mankind, is the power of communicating their thoughts to one another. Destitute of this power, Reason would be a solitary, and, in some measure, an unavailing principle. Speech is the great instrument by which man becomes beneficial to man: and it is to the intercourse and transmission of thought, by means of speech, that we are chiefly indebted for the improvement of thought itself.
>
> (Blair, *Lectures*, vol. I, p. 1)

POETS AND ORATORS

Arts of rhetoric have always drawn heavily on literature for illustrative examples, quotations from the poets and playwrights having the advantage of being concise, memorable, and perhaps already familiar. More important, rhetoric has freely acknowledged the poets as pioneers and paragons: Homer used levels of style in order to differentiate characters (Quintilian, II. xvii. 8), while Virgil eventually came to be regarded as at once the supreme orator and the supreme poet, hence too the supreme teacher of rhetorical art, the master of Dante (E. R. Curtius, *European Literature*, pp. 356–7).

The fusion of rhetoric and poetry was made easier by a steady widening of the definition of rhetoric during the classical period. By a characteristically ethical argument, turning on Socrates' refusal to sacrifice virtue to expediency at his trial, Quintilian proves that 'the end which the orator must keep in view is not persuasion, but speaking well' ('bene dicendi': XI. i. 11). By the time of the Renaissance this enlarged definition was well-nigh standard. Abraham Fraunce begins by announcing that 'Rhetorike is an Art of speaking' (*Arcadian Rhetorike*, 1588, p. 3), and proceeds to show that it is the art of speaking artistically. Cicero would not have gone so far, though his desire to establish differences between poetry and rhetoric indicates how they were already coming together. They have, as he admits, a great deal in common: 'the poet is a very near kinsman of the orator, rather more heavily fettered as regards rhythm, but with ampler freedom in his choice of words [archaisms, bolder metaphors, and so on], while in the use of many sorts of ornament he is his ally and almost his counterpart' (*De Oratore*, I. xvi. 70). Cicero does not abandon the idea of persuasion, but he concedes that the orator has other duties too: 'The supreme orator, then, is the one whose speech instructs, delights, and moves the minds of his audience [*et docet et delectat et permovet*]. The orator is in duty bound to instruct; giving pleasure is a free gift to the audience, to move them is indispensable' (*De Optimo Genere Oratorum*, 3). This is very like Horace's view of the poet's task, which is to move his audience, especially if he is a dramatic poet, and to blend profit with pleasure (*Ars Poetica*, 99ff., 333 ff.). In the Renaissance, Horace's precepts are put into Ciceronian dress: 'the functions of the poet are that he should teach well, that he should delight, and that he should move. . . .' (Minturno, *L'Arte Poetica* (1564), in Allan H. Gilbert, *Literary Criticism: Plato to Dryden* (New York, 1940), p. 297).

Having learnt from poetry, especially in stylistic matters, rhetoric accepted the poets as its apt and ready pupils. Curtius sees Ovid as the key figure, and claims the transference of rhetoric to Roman poetry as his accomplishment (*European Literature*, p. 66). Certainly, Ovid's adoption of rhetorical forms and styles is whole-hearted, the influence of rhetorical education very plain. One of his favourite forms is the *prosopopoeia*, the dramatic monologue of a legendary or historical character. Another is the poetic equivalent of the *chria*, the careful elaboration of an ethical theme. And in a verse epistle to Salanus, a teacher of rhetoric, he is quite explicit about the relationship between the two arts:

> Our work differs, but it derives from the same sources; we are both worshippers of liberal art . . . there should be fire in us both: as my numbers receive vigour from your eloquence, so I lend brilliance to your words. By right then you think my poetry connected with your pursuit and you believe that the rites of our common warfare should be preserved.
>
> (*Ex Ponto*, II. v. 65 ff.)

In the Middle Ages the identity of rhetoric and poetry was virtually complete. Ciceronian doctrines could easily be converted into poetical theory, and most 'Arts of Poetry' in this period are in fact arts of rhetoric with additional material on versification. The most authoritative was the early thirteenth-century *Poetria*

Nova of Geoffrey of Vinsauf (the 'Gaufred, deere maister sover-ayn' of the *Nun's Priest's Tale*) which discusses the poet's task under the heads of Invention, Arrangement and Style, giving most weight to the last. The result of this tendency is the sort of con-flation which Erasmus welcomed: 'What especially delights me is a rhetorical poem and a poetical oration, in which you can see the poetry in the prose and the rhetorical expression in the poetry' (Letter to Andrew Ammonius, 21 December 1513; cited in Vickers, *Francis Bacon*, p. 289). Later we find George Puttenham making the necessary discriminations – poetry, unlike oratory, involves imitation and uses metre – but emphasizing that the poet is, properly speaking, the best kind of rhetorician: 'the Poet is of all other the most auncient Orator, as he that by good and pleasant perswasions first reduced the wilde and beastly people into pub-licke societies and civilitie of life, insinuating unto them, under fictions with sweete and coloured speeches, many wholesome lessons and doctrines. ...' 'So as the Poets were also from the beginning the best perswaders and their eloquence the first Rhetoricke of the world' (*Arte of English Poesie*, pp. 196 and 8).

SOME FORMS AND TOPICS

Rhetoric was often represented during the Middle Ages as a tall and beautiful lady. Her robes are sumptuously adorned with the figures of speech, and in her hand she carries weapons with which to wound her adversaries. These weapons are wielded in judicial rhetoric, and in demonstrative orations which are devoted to censure and condemnation. Literary satire is closely related to both of these. The satirist, like the orator, is entering a protest in public, addressing an audience with a view to changing its attitudes and disturbing its complacency. In satires with a strong frame-work of logic and argument, or in which the author offers an apologia for his muse and his career, elements of judicial oratory, especially techniques of proof and refutation, may be relevant. Besides *vituperatio*, the attack on wicked and unworthy individuals, satire will also adopt loftier rhetorical ends: dissuasion from vice and folly, and praise of those whose example deserves to be followed. We know that Juvenal, who had been trained in one of the Roman schools of declamation, was a pleader before he turned satirist. Dryden, too, would have learned to declaim, and indeed to declaim satirically, as a schoolboy at Westminster.

Ethical works which aim explicitly to persuade us to virtue's cause, and didactic poems offering practical instruction, are other 'kinds' in which literature and rhetoric co-operate. The hand of rhetoric is also seen in the epistolary form in which many poetical persuasions, from Horace onwards, have been cast. Since it is addressed to a specific audience, though an audience only of one, the private letter was even in Roman times regarded as part of the rhetorician's province. Boys were given practice in writing letters from imaginary persons, so that they would enlarge their imaginative experience and learn appropriateness of style. This was a variant of *prosopopoeia*, and bears fruit in Ovid's heroical epistles. In the twelfth century the prestige of the letter increased very rapidly, with its growing use in administration and politics. Guidance was provided by the *Artes Dictamini* (or *Dictandi*), which furnished models for official letters and documents. The Renaissance developed this tendency by stressing the importance of private correspondence as a vehicle of persuasion. Letters were defined as miniature orations, and classified according to the three types of oratory. So the letter of condolence could be seen as a personal and abbreviated form of the *consolatio*, the consolatory oration which is both a memorial tribute and a dissuasion from fruitless mourning. Erasmus, who took the epistolary art very seriously, advised that the 'deliberative' letter should follow the structure of the formal speech, and put his own advice into practice in a letter persuading a young gentleman to marry (translated in Wilson's *Rhetorique*, pp. 39–63). And to the three-fold classification he added an important new genre, the familiar letter, of the kind for which models are sometimes still found in books of etiquette. Here the *ars dictamini* enters the history of the novel. Samuel Richardson, commissioned to write a volume of familiar letters, became so imaginatively engaged in the predicament of one of his 'correspondents' that he began, almost accidentally, to create the first major epistolary novel.

Meanwhile other forms shaped or inspired by rhetoric had established themselves. The demonstrative oration influenced the poetical panegyric, the poem in praise of a king or a mistress. Milton's 'L'Allegro' and 'Il Penseroso' are poems celebrating contrasted attitudes, or (according to E. M. W. Tillyard) the respective merits of day and night. They also reflect the form of the disputation or debate, an educational exercise which was considered especially valuable in legal training, and whose impact on English literature can be traced as early as the twelfth-century poem *The Owl and the Nightingale*. In the sixteenth century the debate was absorbed into the dramatic interlude and the morality play. To take a final example: it has been suggested that Aristotle's discussion of commonplaces and maxims helped to establish the cultivation of the moral aphorism, or *pensée*, in the seventeenth century (Croll, *Style, Rhetoric, and Rhythm*, p. 135).

Rhetorical education was also responsible for the widespread dissemination of the topics and commonplaces as a body of material common to orators and poets alike. This material formed an important part of the general cultural tradition, a stock of ideas that was freely drawn upon throughout the 'Latin Middle Ages' (as E. R. Curtius calls it) and later. Curtius has shown how the topics persisted as 'clichés, which can be used in any form of literature', and how they 'spread to all spheres of life with which literature deals and to which it gives form' (*European Literature,*

p. 70). The commonplaces and topics, as we have seen, included manners of proceeding and forms of argument that could serve a variety of oratorical purposes. One such is the topic of modesty, the assumed humility of the orator faced with a difficult case or a formidable opponent. The speaker hesitates at the opening of his speech, confessing his inexperience and lack of ability, and so obtains a favourable hearing. In literary use the modesty formula appears in the stock excuse that the author has only reluctantly agreed to publish his work, encouraged by his patron or pressed by his friends. The opening of *Lycidas* makes direct use of the plea of inexperience; the opening of *Paradise Lost* combines the orator's call to attention ('Things unattempted yet in Prose or Rhime') with the true humility of prayer.

Another favoured rhetorical argument is to consider the possibility or impossibility of an action. This is obviously most relevant in a judicial speech, but as a school exercise in demonstrative oratory pupils might try their hand at rehearsing a series of fantastic impossibilities. Such catalogues then make their way into poetry. The lyric poet may prove the enduring nature of his passion by such an argument: 'Till a' the seas gang dry, my Dear, And the rocks melt wi' the sun. . . .' Or the despairing lover, seeing his beloved favour some lucky rival, may envisage similarly undreamt-of occurrences in the natural world – griffins mating with mares, the oak bearing golden apples (Virgil, *Eclogue* VIII).

Curtius has argued that through such ethical commonplaces as 'virtue is the true nobility' classical rhetoric handed on to the Middle Ages and the Renaissance the wisdom and ideals of antiquity. Undoubtedly such topics are experienced afresh and redefined by succeeding ages, but an essential continuity is preserved. So it is too with descriptive topics like the *locus amoenus*, the delightful scene, the ideal landscape of flowery meadow, purling brook, and cooling shades which features in a hundred pastoral poems, romances and dream-visions. Spenser incorporated its elements, but with his own moral emphasis, in the Bower of Bliss. One of Curtius' points is that the absorption of so much classical material, from direct imitation of models and from the continuity of topics, led to an easy assimilation of pagan and Christian, so that the Christian poet or public speaker could assume without embarrassment the terminology of the Roman Pantheon. 'As a man and a citizen, one is a Christian; as a rhetor, a pagan' (p. 443). Horace and Virgil could be accommodated to Christian culture, and pagan mythology to the Christian religion – until towards the end of the seventeenth century the compound came to seem artificial, distasteful, and impious.

THE ELIZABETHANS AND AFTER

In the English Renaissance the interrelationship of literature and rhetoric is clearly observed not only in satiric and didactic writings but also in the fields of drama and lyrical poetry. A play, like a sermon, could be organized round a text. Richard Edwards' tragicomedy *Damon and Pithias* (ca. 1565) takes friendship as a theme to be explored and illustrated. Muriel Bradbrook has pointed out how Chapman's tragedy *Caesar and Pompey* is an elaboration of the maxim (printed at the end of the play's 'argument') that 'Only a just man is a free man', a stoic paradox that must frequently have served as the subject of a *chria* or a debate. Chapman seems to have believed that it is the function of an 'authentical tragedy' to excite its audience to virtue and dissuade it from vice (Bradbrook, *Themes and Conventions*, p. 76). In the earlier tragedies attempts at representing inner conflict regularly fall into the inflexible mode of the deliberative oration; the character weighs up the pros and cons of an action before deciding what to do next. Gradually the rigidities of rhetoric were relaxed, so that the soliloquy revealed the speaker's thoughts as they

E

occurred, rather than as they were predetermined by the dramatist. Meanwhile the subtler possibilities of figured speech were being investigated. In Kyd's *Spanish Tragedy* the schemes of rhetoric are used to reveal character. The ineffectual, courtly Balthazar, who expresses himself readily in the artificial modes of repetition and *gradatio*, is put in his place by the scornful interruptions of Lorenzo, the down-to-earth plain-spoken Machiavel. Shakespeare carried these possibilities still further. In *Much Ado about Nothing*, as Brian Vickers has pointed out, the villain Don John speaks a formalized, symmetrical prose: 'I am trusted with a muzzle and enfranchised with a clog. . . . If I had my mouth, I would bite; if I had my liberty, I would do my liking.' This establishes the rigidity of his 'uncompromising egoism' and ruthlessness, and contrasts markedly with the freer exchanges we have witnessed between the more socially attuned characters (*Artistry of Shakespeare's Prose*, pp. 177 ff.).

Accustomed as we are to thinking of the lyric as an expression, or outpouring, of emotion, we may be unwilling to allow rhetoric to have anything to do with it. But such an attitude would imply an unwarrantable restriction of the lyric's scope. Many a short Elizabethan poem is a scaled-down demonstrative oration, a panegyric on the lady's beauty and virtue, or an ingenious mock-censure: 'My mistress' eyes are nothing like the sun. . . .' An obvious case is the April eclogue in Spenser's *Shepheardes Calender*. The poem's Argument announces that it is 'purposely intended to the honor and prayse of our most gracious sovereigne', suitably referred to as 'Elisa, Queene of shepheardes all'. E. K.'s gloss reminds us of the poem's decorum, shows how the poet uses the topics of praise (for example, the lady's ancestry), and points to the exordium, narration, and conclusion as they occur.

The lyric poet could also write persuasively, in the deliberative or even the judicial manner. Puttenham pleasantly ridicules the plight of love-poets:

the poore soules sometimes praying, beseeching, sometime honour-
ing, avancing [extolling], praising: an other while railing, reviling,
and cursing: then sorrowing, weeping, lamenting: in the ende
laughing, rejoysing and solacing the beloved againe, with a thousand
delicate devises, odes, songs, elegies, ballads, sonets and other ditties,
mooving one way and another to great compassion.

(Arte of English Poesie, p. 45)

The poet is most often trying to arouse the lady's pity and to melt
her hostility or indifference, but he may also need to confute the
arguments of adversaries, rivals or bystanders. Many of Donne's
lyrics are persuasive in this very direct way, as 'The Flea' and the
'Valediction forbidding Mourning,' whose title at once reveals its
explicitly rhetorical purpose. Its argument-through-imagery is
designed to convince the lady of the superior quality of their love,
while the celebrated compass image introduces a topic of praise
('Thy firmnes makes my circle just') which puts mourning out of
the question; for if so much depends on her stability of character,
it becomes impossible for her to burst into tears.

Again, the poet may argue with himself, persuading or half-
persuading himself to a course of action, as in sonnet 47 of Sidney's
Astrophil and Stella:

> What, have I thus betrayed my libertie?
>   Can those blacke beames such burning markes engrave
>   In my free side? or am I borne a slave,
> Whose necke becomes such yoke of tyranny?
> Or want I sense to feele my miserie?
>   Or sprite, disdaine of such disdaine to have?
>   Who for long faith, tho dayly helpe I crave,
> May get no almes but scorne of beggerie.
>   Vertue awake, Beautie but beautie is,
> I may, I must, I can, I will, I do
>   Leave following that, which it is gaine to misse.
> Let her go. Soft, but here she comes. Go to,
>   Unkind, I love you not: O me, that eye
>   Doth make my heart give to my tongue the lie.

The opening battery of questions (*quaesitio*) gives dramatic force to the poet's surprise and indignation at having *thus* betrayed his liberty, and the intensity of his feelings is reinforced by alliteration and repetitions that suggest a growing firmness of purpose: 'disdaine of such disdaine to have'; 'Beautie but beautie is'. The line 'I may, I must, I can, I will, I do' employs *anaphora* and *parison*, and arranges its verbs in a carefully climactic sequence (*auxesis* or *incrementum*, translated by Puttenham as 'the avancer or figure of encrease'). We do not have to wait until the end of the poem to see that the huffing will all be in vain. The contrivance of the rhetoric, especially the heavy tread of the *incrementum* figure, calls attention to itself just enough to show that the poet is protesting too much, trying to work up a determination he cannot quite feel. As the final line admits, his heart is not in his oratory. Yet the overthrow of the elaborate self-persuasive rhetoric is part of a larger rhetorical aim. The purpose of the sonnet is to acknowledge, and to persuade the reader to acknowledge, Stella's beauty and the irresistible power of love.

The case of Sir Philip Sidney is an instructive one. He was a master of rhetorical skill, a virtuoso of the schemes. In Abraham Fraunce's *Arcadian Rhetorike* each of the figures is illustrated by a quotation from Sidney's poetry or prose. Yet with a restraint developed by true imitation of the classics, perhaps too by the Ramist insistence on logical control, he avoided the merely decorative in favour of an intelligent and dramatic use of the figures which would express the 'forcibleness or *energia* (as the Greeks call it) of the writer' (*Apology*, ed. Shepherd, p. 38). The figures are means to the poet's greater end, which is to reveal the truth and to win men's minds to virtue. And the figures are also subservient to decorum, the stylistic quality on which all Renaissance critics insist. For Puttenham, as for Cicero, decorum was almost a way of life. For Milton it was 'the grand masterpiece to observe' in all poetical writing (*Of Education*), while Dryden was a firm believer in literary propriety: 'in the heightenings of poetry, the strength and vehemence of figures should be suited to the occasion, the subject and the persons' (Preface to *The Spanish Friar* (1681), *Essays*, vol. I, p. 278). Figures should also be suited to the chosen level of style, the grand, the middle, or the plain. In turn these stylistic levels help to determine the hierarchy of literary 'kinds': pastoral, satire and burlesque are humble forms for which the low style is fitting; most odes and lyrics, and some types of elegy, occupy a middle ground; tragic, heroic and sacred poetry, being the most exalted genres, demand the loftiest style. The theory of 'kinds' remained unshaken until the mid-eighteenth century, since the poets, most of whom had had an education centred upon rhetoric, were content to write within this framework. Dryden, for instance, had been thoroughly trained in the rhetorical disciplines at Westminster School under Richard Busby. As one mother proudly wrote in 1688: 'They are bravely taught both to be scholars and orators at Doctor Busby's school at Westminster, where my son is' (G. F. Russell Barker, *Memoir of Richard Busby*, London, 1895, p. 100). In much of his poetry, and in many of his plays, Dryden and his characters are to be found pleading a case or arguing a cause; and his critical principles bear the unmistakeable stamp of Roman rhetorical theory.

By way of a very brief illustration of the interrelationships of rhetoric and poetry after 1700 we may glance at Pope, whose work was among the first to which modern criticism began to apply rhetorical criteria; at the poems of Johnson, with their deeply serious, functional use of the figures of words (repetition and parallelism) and of thought (exemplum and emphasis); and at *The Deserted Village*, in which Goldsmith appeals to poetry not to forsake its didactic, rhetorical role:

> Aid slighted truth, with thy persuasive strain
> Teach erring man to spurn the rage of gain.

(423–4)

As for later poets, it was inevitable that Hopkins, with his strong conviction that poetry must be heard, should look to rhetoric for help in building aural patterns through which to express his meanings:

> This seeing the sick endears them to us, us too it endears.
> My tongue had taught thee comfort, touch had quenched thy tears,
> Thy tears that touched my heart, child, Felix, poor Felix Randal.

Hopkins deserved an exuberant 'E.K.' to exclaim over his *adnominatio* (a word repeated as a different part of speech or in a different grammatical case: 'touch/touched'), and the *chiasmus* of 'endears them to us, us too it endears' – an example that more nearly approaches symmetry, through the homophony of *to* and *too*, when the line is read aloud. But the major part of this E. K.'s task would be to comment on the aptness of the figures, here linking and locking together the poet and the farrier, the sick man and the ministering priest.

It was also inevitable that T. S. Eliot, exploring the possibilities of musical organization in poetry, should create verbal patterns which hark back to the schemes and figures:

> Keeping time,
> Keeping the rhythm in their dancing
> As in their living in the living seasons
> The time of the seasons and the constellations
> The time of milking and the time of harvest
> The time of the coupling of man and woman
> And that of beasts. Feet rising and falling.
> Eating and drinking. Dung and death.
>
> (*Four Quartets*, East Coker)

Since 1700 the literature of persuasion has continued to flourish in prose. The rhetorician manipulates us in the polemical prose of Swift at one end of the eighteenth century, in Burke and the author of the Junius Letters at the other; and in Ruskin and Carlyle and

Arnold. We find him entering the novel too, in the pages of Fielding, Sterne, and Scott, above all in Dickens, the great master of 'auditory prose', of prose like the orator's, written to be heard. The description of the burning of Newgate in *Barnaby Rudge* provides a model example of the figure *demonstratio*, and Cicero would have extolled the rhythms of its periods. Most important, the rhetorical devices compel us to face the terrible irony of a liberty that may be worse than imprisonment:

> Now, now, the door was down. Now they came rushing through the jail, calling to each other in the vaulted passages; clashing the iron gates dividing yard from yard; beating at the doors of cells and wards; wrenching off bolts and locks and bars; tearing down the doorposts to get men out; endeavouring to drag them by main force through gaps and windows where a child could scarcely pass. . . . Anon some famished wretch whose theft had been a loaf of bread, or scrap of butcher's meat, came skulking past, barefooted, – going slowly away because that jail, his house, was burning; not because he had any other, or had friends to meet, or old haunts to revisit, or any liberty to gain, but liberty to starve and die.
>
> (ch. 65)

The set pieces in Dickens' novels demand the kind of impassioned public recital that their author himself used to give.

5
The Renunciation
of Rhetoric

Among the senses of the word *rhetoric* listed in the *Oxford English Dictionary* is the following: 'Speech or writing expressed in terms calculated to persuade; hence (often in depreciatory sense), language characterized by artificial or ostentatious expression.' It is clear from the *Dictionary*'s illustrative quotations that the depreciatory sense was firmly established by the beginning of the seventeenth century. In 1615 Richard Brathwait could scornfully dismiss the work of contemporary poetasters with the jibe: 'Heere is no substance, but a simple peece/Of gaudy Rhetoricke.' In 1642 Thomas Fuller observed that some people 'condemn Rhetorick as the mother of lies'.

These quotations helpfully isolate two main reasons, one aesthetic, the other moral, why rhetoric came to acquire a bad name. The moral attack we have already seen in Plato's *Gorgias*. To condemn rhetoric as the mother of lies is to take up basically the Socratic position: rhetoric distorts and conceals the truth. Conversely, it can give evil thoughts an alluring aspect. For if rhetoric is the mother of lies it follows that she is Satan's helpmate. Milton's Satan, like all his tempters, is a great maker of speeches, pre-eminent even among the skilful orators of Hell. It is in introducing one of these, Belial, that Milton presents the classic formulation of the moral case against rhetoric:

> A fairer person lost not Heav'n; he seemd
> For dignity compos'd and high exploit:
> But all was false and hollow; though his Tongue

Dropt Manna, and could make the worse appear
The better reason, to perplex and dash
Maturest Counsels: for his thoughts were low. ...
(Paradise Lost, II, 110–15)

Not that Milton renounces rhetoric; rather the opposite, since the verbal organization of his poems is rich and complex. He requires only that our moral censure should fall on the character and motive of the immoral orator. This is the Aristotelian reply to Socrates: we cannot hold rhetoric responsible for the evil uses to which it is put by the unscrupulous or the flippant. None the less, it is easy to allow our condemnation of the sinful ends of the speaker to attach itself to the neutral means he employs, and this nagging sense of the moral unworthiness of rhetoric has given increased point and force to criticisms made on other grounds.

In Brathwait's antithesis of 'substance' and 'gaudy rhetoric' we can see the beginnings of an opposition between real thought and insubstantial ornament. Among the historical factors promoting this attitude must be counted the Ramist separation of dialectic from rhetoric. An unintended consequence of the Ramist reform was the strengthening of the rhetoricians' tendency to concentrate on stylistic matters, even to equate rhetoric with style. Verbal dexterity has always been the pitfall of the orator. In the second century A.D., Lucian gave an ironic recipe for rhetorical success, based on the worst contemporary practice: exaggeration and free use of cliché, extravagant gestures and plenty of linguistic tricks. The facile imitation of Cicero's style in the sixteenth century was censured by Erasmus, Ramus, and Gabriel Harvey; and by Bacon, who in *The Advancement of Learning* complains that choice phrases are preferred to weighty subjects and sound arguments. The nub of his criticism is that those who follow this modish trend are hunting more after words than matter.

Bacon thus reintroduces the problem of *res* and *verba.* His impatience with ornate verbiage and his emphasis on 'matter' is shared by Montaigne: 'Away with that Eloquence that so enchants us with its Harmony, that we should more study it than things' ('A Consideration upon Cicero', *Essays*, trans. Charles Cotton, 3rd ed., 1700, vol. I, p. 397). Significantly Montaigne prefers the Spartans, who 'made it their Business to enquire into things', to the Athenians, who simply 'cudgell'd their Brains about Words' ('Of Pedantry', vol. I, p. 210), while the sort of author-reader relationship fostered by rhetoric is repellent to him: 'I would not have an Author make it his business to render Me attentive' ('Of Books', vol. II, p. 133). The 'things' and 'matter' to which Bacon and Montaigne refer include all those phenomena that the practical scientist will wish to investigate. The emergence of the scientific spirit of enquiry, with its scepticism and its distrust of established authority, helped to weaken the hold of rhetoric even more. The educational discipline of imitation was beginning to give way to the ideal of growth and progress through discovery. The Royal Society even proposed a new standard of prose style, especially suitable for scientific reports and discussions, a style that deliberately eschewed ornament. According to Thomas Sprat, the Society's first historian, its members sought 'to return back to the primitive Purity and Shortness, when Men deliver'd so many *Things*, almost in an equal Number of *Words*' (*History of the Royal Society*, 1667, p. 113).

Behind this reforming zeal lies a distrust, even a fear, of words. The controversies and hostilities of the seventeenth century are blamed on language, and therefore on rhetoric. Irresponsible oratory was held to have fanned the destructive passions of the Civil War and to have encouraged nonconformist 'enthusiasm' or fanaticism. After the Restoration, preachers and politicians are urged to avoid ornament and appeals to the passions. Metaphor is a snare and a delusion. Such an attitude was not altogether new – the original court of justice in Athens, the Areopagus, had tried to forbid eloquence in cases tried before it – but it was buttressed in the late seventeenth century by fears of a renewal of civil conflict, by the scientists' elevation of 'doing' over 'talking', and by the authority of the philosopher John Locke. Locke is certain that the chief end of language is communication; that figurative language tends to impede communication by introducing ambiguities and irrelevant emotions; that it constitutes, therefore, one of the abuses of language and must be pruned away. Not much can be said on behalf of rhetoric: 'we must allow, that all the Art of Rhetorick, besides [i.e. apart from] Order and Clearness, all the artificial and figurative application of Words Eloquence hath invented, are for nothing else but to insinuate wrong *Ideas*, move the Passions, and thereby mislead the Judgment; and so indeed are perfect cheat' (*An Essay concerning Humane Understanding*, 4th ed., 1700, Book III, ch. x, p. 301). Reluctantly, Locke admits that rhetoric is popular – but this only goes to show that men take a perverse delight in being deceived.

As far as prose communication is concerned, something at least is left for rhetoric to attend to – the qualities of clarity and orderliness. The classically-minded could comfort themselves that Quintilian had set great store by just these virtues. He considered 'clearness as the first essential of a good style' (VIII. ii. 22). 'We must study not only that every hearer may understand us, but that it shall be impossible for him not to understand us' (VIII. ii. 24; Blair's translation, *Lectures*, vol. I, p. 185). In the realm of poetry eloquence was still something to be valued. Grammar school and university education remained an education in the classics; the orators continued to be studied, and rhetorical exercises to be prescribed. *The Spectator* reveals very clearly the state of uneasy truce that had been reached by the early years of the eighteenth century. In its pages 'eloquence' and 'oratory' are terms of approval, but 'rhetorician' has become distinctly pejorative, and the derogatory phrase 'the pomp of rhetoric' is already something of a cliché.

Later in the century the rigidity of literary-rhetorical theory was further shaken. The dividing lines between the 'kinds' of literature were crossed by the writers of bourgeois tragedy and sentimental comedy. If the genres go into the melting-pot they take decorum with them; stylistic decorum is deprived of its *raison d'être* if there is nothing for it to be clearly appropriate to. At the same time the whole conception of poetry was changing. It was no longer considered a public art, to be judged by external criteria of moral responsibility (like rhetoric), but intensely private, seeking no ulterior end, and morally autonomous. Its end is not communication but self-communing. John Stuart Mill made this distinction very clearly in his essay 'What is Poetry?' of 1833:

> Poetry and eloquence are both alike the expression or uttering forth of feeling. But if we may be excused the seeming affectation of the antithesis, we should say that eloquence is *heard*, poetry is *over*heard. Eloquence supposes an audience; the peculiarity of poetry appears to us to lie in the poet's utter unconsciousness of a listener. Poetry is feeling confessing itself to itself, in moments of solitude. . . .
>
> All poetry is of the nature of soliloquy. . . . What we have said to ourselves, we may tell to others afterwards. . . . But no trace of consciousness that any eyes are upon us must be visible in the work itself.
>
> (*Mill's Essays on Literature and Society*,
> ed. J. B. Schneewind, New York, 1965, p. 109)

For Mill a 'public poetry' was a contradiction in terms. 'True poetry' (though we might ask where true poetry, corresponding to Mill's definition, is actually to be found) was now divorced from rhetoric, whose fortunes were at a very low ebb.

They were to sink still lower, however, under the vigorous onslaught of Benedetto Croce, the Italian philosopher and critic. Croce was the implacable enemy of all classifying into genres, all division and separation (for example, of means from ends) in the world of art. Unity was his cry, the indivisibility of artistic 'intuition' and artistic expression. In his *Aesthetic* (1901) he maintains that rhetoric is a contaminated art because it takes into account factors, such as the presence of the audience, with which the true artist has nothing to do. But rhetoric is chiefly pernicious because it drives a wedge between the great inseparables, style and form, content and expression. Croce attacks rhetoric as an inadequate doctrine of style, a 'theory of ornate form' postulating a process of composition in which ornament is superadded to a bare and unadorned statement. Style is not crudely applied ornament, Croce insists, in spite of rhetorical teaching to the contrary. He notes in passing that the 'theory of ornate form' received support from the habit of using Latin for literary and educational purposes. When an author is writing in a dead language he inclines to see his craft in terms of manipulating words from outside rather than feeling them on his pulses. Croce maintains that as a theory of art rhetoric is worse than useless. Its shortcomings are exposed by 'the very nature of aesthetic activity, which does not lend itself to partition; there is no such thing as activity of type *a* or type *b*, nor can the same concept be expressed now in one way, now in another' (*Aesthetic*, p. 436).

The rhetorical habit of systematizing and classifying, though it has facilitated the transmission of the rules from textbook to textbook, has not been an unmixed blessing. R. R. Bolgar has argued that the writing of character-sketches and similar rhetorical exercises fostered a tendency to see human beings in terms of limited stereotypes; rhetoric may thus have helped to cramp the development of classical ideas on psychology and ethics (*Classical Heritage*, pp. 38-9). The forms of rhetoric have also been found unadaptable and limiting in debate and controversy. The case has been well stated by Richard Lanham, who observes that the primary assumption of rhetorical form 'is that all arguments are or can be polar opposites . . . and it does violence to any issue that falls into the "both-and" rather than the "either-or" category. It can offer a form for argument, that is, but not for compromise. How many compromises, it is then reasonable to ask, have been hindered by the *form?*' (*Handlist of Rhetorical Terms*, p. 113). The currently fashionable word 'dialogue', and the even more fashionable phrase 'continuing dialogue' indicate a marked and proper preference for more flexible forms of discussion which do not put obstacles in the way of compromise but attempt to accommodate divergent points of view.

Finally, it must be admitted that the rhetoricians have sometimes been rhetoric's worst enemies. In the nineteenth century they not unnaturally began to show an increasing lack of confidence about the role and significance of their teaching, and their manuals became in consequence repetitive and cautious. I. A. Richards lampoons Bishop Whately's advice on style, but his strictures could apply elsewhere: 'Instead of a philosophic inquiry into how words work in discourse, we get the usual postcard's worth of crude common sense:– be clear, yet don't be dry . . . respect usage; don't be long-winded, on the other hand don't be gaspy . . .' (*Philosophy of Rhetoric*, p. 8).

The combined effect of all these factors is clearly visible in the derogatory uses of 'rhetoric' that were cited in the first chapter. Rhetoric becomes morally suspect, if not actually reprehensible. It is applied ornament, the art of the purple passage and the debating trick, language masquerading as thought. It begins to seem that rhetoric has been driven back once and for all to its original preserves, or their modern equivalents: the pulpit and the law court, the political platform and the lecture-room.

6
Rhetoric Renewed

Croce realized that rhetoric was too dangerous to be left to expire in peace. The 'rhetorical categories' should continue to appear in school curricula, he declared, so that they can be kept under constant critical scrutiny. 'The errors of the past must not be forgotten. ... Unless an account of the rhetorical categories be given, accompanied by a criticism of them, there is a risk of their springing up again' (*Aesthetic*, pp. 72–3). It was this kind of account and critique which I. A. Richards undertook in his *Philosophy of Rhetoric* (1936). Richards has much in common with Croce. He is quite as firmly opposed to any crude separation of form and content, and to the sort of 'wretchedly inconvenient metaphor' that refers to language as the dress of thought. Again, he rejects what he calls the Proper Meaning Superstition, the belief, underlying many traditional accounts of metaphor, that a word can be said to have a 'proper meaning' which exists in the abstract, independently of the actual uses of that word (pp. 11–12). Unlike Croce, however, Richards is reconstructing rhetoric, building a new rhetoric to replace the old. For Richards the old rhetoric was 'the theory of the battle of words'; its teaching and rules were 'dominated by the combative impulse', by the need to convince, and to win cases. It was the weapon of controversy, and 'a controversy is normally an exploitation of a systematic set of misunderstandings for war-like purposes' (p. 39). The new rhetoric, far from taking mean advantage of the obstacles that beset clear communication, is 'a study of misunderstanding *and its remedies*' (p. 3; my italics). And the new rhetorician does not wield a Lockean pruning-knife. His task is rather to attend closely to the meaning and behaviour of words in their contexts, and this involves attending to ambiguity. Here Richards clearly parts company with the traditional view of ambiguity as a vice of style, producing obscurity, or as a clever technique for gaining a laugh. For Richards ambiguity is a natural property of language, 'the indispensable means of most of our most important utterances – especially in Poetry and Religion' (p. 40).

The re-defined rhetoric plays a central role in Richards' poetic theory, since he regards literature as primarily a transaction between author and reader. His work has encouraged an emphasis on the element of 'discourse' in literature, as among the American New Critics and others, and a renewed interest in the way in which a poem works. The impact of this revived rhetoric on literary criticism has already been suggested. Didactic and overtly persuasive writings, especially satirical and polemical works, have been re-assessed. Detailed studies have been undertaken of the 'means of persuading' used by individual poets and dramatists. The novelist's techniques for presenting experience to his readers, his ways of 'telling', 'showing', and dramatizing, have been investigated, notably in Wayne Booth's *Rhetoric of Fiction*. Booth takes as his subject 'the rhetorical resources available to the writer of epic, novel, or short story as he tries, consciously or unconsciously, to impose his fictional world upon the reader'. This sounds almost like a modified version of Aristotle's definition of rhetoric – except for the word 'unconsciously'. That adverb serves to mollify those like Croce who fear that if the artist has even half an eye on his audience his intuitive vision will be impaired. Booth maintains that 'the success of an author's rhetoric does not depend on whether he thought about his readers as he wrote; if "mere calculation" cannot insure success, it is equally true that even the most unconscious and Dionysian of writers succeeds only if he makes us join in the dance' (Preface). Like Richards, Booth recognizes the control which an author exercises over his reader's thoughts and feelings. We are reminded of Dr Johnson's assertion: 'That book is good in vain which the reader throws away. He only is the master who keeps the mind in pleasing captivity' ('Life of Dryden'). Johnson too insisted that literature is a transaction between the author and his public. The man who writes for himself alone cannot complain if he finds no readers.

Our growing knowledge of the historical ties between literature and rhetoric has also prompted critical studies along more traditionally rhetorical lines. The structure of the classical oration has been discovered in Sidney's *Apology for Poetry* and in Dryden's *Astraea Redux*; schemes of organization deriving from classical rhetoric have been traced in Bacon's works; the function and importance of the figures have been investigated in works as different as *Paradise Lost* and *Tristram Shandy*. Such studies have raised the very practical question of nomenclature. Detailed and comprehensive analysis of the figures requires the handling of terms more esoteric than those, like alliteration and hyperbole, to which we are accustomed. Our difficulty in distinguishing, say, an *interrogatio* from a *percontatio*, is not made any easier by a lack of agreement among the advocates of rhetoric as to the precise meaning of some of the terms they use, and as to the most suitable labels for the figures; some critics prefer Greek forms (*auxesis, epiplexis*), some their Latin equivalents (*incrementum, percontatio*), and some a mixture of the two. When the problem was aired some years ago in the pages of *Essays in Criticism*, Donald Davie argued that a large-scale adoption of rhetorical terminology would 'rule out the common reader altogether, and make academic criticism entirely a closed shop', though he conceded that a knowledge of rhetorical terms might make it easier to talk about figures or patterns which the 'common reader' has noticed but to which he cannot give a convenient name.

On this view, the terms have at least the merit of serving as a kind of critical shorthand. But on any view they cannot be accepted as substitutes for critical examination of particular effects in particular works by particular authors. We are not greatly helped by being told, for example, that alliteration is to be found in *The Faerie Queene*, *Absalom and Achitophel*, and *The Rime of the Ancient Mariner*. Only if we turn to those texts can we discover what the figure alliteration is actually capable of, what variety of tones and feelings it can be used to convey. In a valuable section of his recent study, *Classical Rhetoric in English Poetry*, Brian Vickers does exactly this: he cites and comments on remarkably varied examples of the basic formula of *antimetabole* from, among others, Montaigne, Overbury, Sterne and Conrad (pp. 120–1). If the uses of the same figure can be so diverse, then the point of contact between them – the formal structure of the figure – is too slight to be of much significance for the critic. (Its value as material for linguistic analysis is a slightly different matter.) Traditional hostility to rhetoric has made much of the inability of formal descriptions of the figures to explain literary or indeed oratorical effects, and has gleefully consigned the hard names to oblivion:

> For all a Rhetoricians Rules
> Teach nothing but to name his Tools.
> (Samuel Butler, *Hudibras*, Part I, canto i, 89–90)

The rhetorician can reply that it is no disadvantage to know the names of the things one is talking about, provided that exalted claims are not made for such knowledge. And that an approach to a literary text which begins by examining the figures at work has the not inconsiderable merit of starting with the precise organization of the words on the printed page. The student of the figures has to be a very careful reader.

He will be a reader, too, whose attention will be focused on the poem rather than on the poet. Rosemond Tuve has strenuously insisted that in reading Elizabethan and Metaphysical poetry we should bring to bear a 'criterion of rhetorical efficacy'. We should think of the poetry not as expressing the author's feelings but as working on the beliefs and emotions of his readers:

> Earlier theory reads as if poetry were conceived of as a relation established between a subject and a reader, though only establishable by a poet. The emphasis on poetry as interesting evidence of the relation between a subject and a particular poet is an emphasis we have learned since, and one which seems the least helpful of any to the understanding of earlier poetry.
>
> (*Elizabethan and Metaphysical Imagery*, p. 189)

Rhetorical theory may certainly help to guard us from any over-simplification of the poet-subject relationship. The Earl of Shaftesbury gave the necessary warning. He quoted Strabo in support of the traditional view that "'tis impossible he shou'd be a great and worthy Poet who is not first a worthy and good Man'; but he went on to claim that as readers we are only entitled to require that the poet 'must at least be *speciously* honest, and *in all appearance* a Friend to Virtue, throughout his Poem' ('Soliloquy: or Advice to an Author,' *Characteristicks*, 2nd ed., 1714, vol. I, pp. 208, 278; Shaftesbury's italics). We cannot argue in a direct line from the artistic effect, the end-product, back to moral or emotional causes. Shaftesbury, that is, requires 'honesty' or virtue in both the poem and the poet, but he sees that this does not necessarily mean an identity of poet with poem, nor even a simple and straightforward relationship between them.

Rhetorical theory has in fact described this relationship in various ways. At one extreme is the amorality of the sophists: the orator is committed to winning his case, irrespective of its merits; his personal beliefs and feelings are irrelevant. At the other extreme we have Blair: 'A writer of genius ... puts on no emotion which his subject does not raise in him; he speaks as he feels; but his style will be beautiful, because his feelings are lively'; and 'we must take care never to counterfeit warmth without feeling it. ...

The heart can only answer to the heart' (*Lectures*, vol. I, p. 365; vol. II, p. 55). The orator must speak in all sincerity or he will fail to sway his audience. Such advice is inevitable when rhetoric includes pulpit oratory. But it holds also for the love-poet. He will persuade his mistress to favour his suit only by persuading her that he is in earnest. His passion, as Sidney realized, will be betrayed by the 'forcibleness or energia' of his poem. In other words, the poet's lively feelings are imaginatively translated into artistic vitality. Between these two extremes comes the doctrine that the orator must sympathize with those on whose behalf he is speaking. He will not experience the same indignation or grief as the man who has actually suffered loss or injustice, but if he is to move his hearers to pity that man he must feel for him with imaginative understanding. He must be at once engaged in his sympathy and detached in his technical control.

All this tends to suggest that the terms and concepts of tradit-ional rhetoric still have a part to play in critical theory and practice. At the humblest level rhetoric provides something to argue against, a solid body of theory which provokes the dissident critic to formulate his own case. W. K. Wimsatt is an outstanding example of a critic who is conversant with rhetorical theory but not content to remain within its boundaries. More positively, we can see a continuity between classical education and modern tech-niques of practical criticism and *explication de texte*. The new disciplines of stylistics and linguistics are investigating many of the areas first surveyed by the rhetoricians – the relationship of *res* and *verba*, or words and things; the problems of translation; the psychological effect of figurative language; the behaviour of words in their contexts – besides the more recent manifestations of persuasive rhetoric in the language of advertising. Geoffrey Leech has written that linguistics is now supplying its own 'descriptive rhetoric' and that the task of stylistics is to 'account for the linguistic features of [a] text in terms of their relevance to literary effect and interpretation' (*Times Literary Supplement*, 23 July 1970). Perhaps the most important continuity of all is that belief in the sanctity of words which has been a recurrent theme in this book. The classical conception of speech as a precious gift of the gods survives in modern injunctions that language must be used and responded to with care, discrimination and moral seriousness.

> Words are the meeting points at which regions of experience which can never combine in sensation or intuition, come together. They are the occasion and the means of that growth which is the mind's endless endeavour to order itself. That is why we have language. It is no mere signalling system. It is the instrument of all our distinctively human development, of everything in which we go beyond the other animals.
>
> (Richards, *Philosophy of Rhetoric*, p. 131)

These are the sentiments and the earnest tone of Isocrates. The words come from the final section of Richards' book, a section which bears as its epigraph a sentence of Henry James, an eloquent reminder of the living importance of rhetoric in its lofty Isocratean sense:

> All life therefore comes back to the question of our speech, the medium through which we communicate with each other; for all life comes back to the question of our relations with each other.
>
> (*The Question of our Speech*, 1905, p. 10)

Bibliography

HISTORY AND TERMINOLOGY

CORBETT, EDWARD P. J. *Classical Rhetoric for the Modern Student.* New York, 1965.

An attempt to bring rhetoric into the classroom. There is a useful rapid survey of the history of rhetoric on pages 535–68.

LANHAM, RICHARD A. *A Handlist of Rhetorical Terms: A Guide for Students of English Literature.* Berkeley and Los Angeles, 1968.

Lively and informative.

PREMINGER, ALEXANDER S. *et al.*, eds. *Encyclopedia of Poetry and Poetics.* Princeton, 1965.

Brief, lucid articles on rhetoric and poetics, style, decorum, invention, amplification, etc.

VICKERS, BRIAN. *Classical Rhetoric in English Poetry.* London, 1970.

Chapters 1 and 2 give an excellent account of the history and processes of rhetoric; chapter 3 considers the functions of the rhetorical figures.

WIMSATT, W. K. and CLEANTH BROOKS. *Literary Criticism: a Short History.* New York and London, 1957.

Especially chapters 4 and 12: the importance of rhetorical theory in classical and neoclassical criticism.

CLASSICAL RHETORIC

(a) Texts

The essential texts, edited and translated, are available in the Loeb Classical Library series (Cambridge, Mass., and London), here abbreviated as 'LCL'.

ARISTOTLE. *The 'Art' of Rhetoric*, trans. J. H. Freese. LCL, 1926. (There is also a very readable translation by R. C. Jebb, ed. J. E. Sandys, Cambridge, 1909.)

CICERO. *De Inventione* and *De Optimo Genere Oratorum* [the latter a brief description of 'the best kind of orator'], trans. H. M. Hubbell. LCL, 1949.

De Oratore (Books I and II), trans. E. W. Sutton and H. Rackham. Revised ed. LCL, 1948.

De Oratore (Book III) and *De Partitione Oratoria*, trans. H. Rackham. LCL, 1942.

Brutus, trans. G. L. Hendrickson, and *Orator*, trans. H. M. Hubbell. Revised ed. LCL, 1962.

Selected Political Speeches, trans. Michael Grant. Harmondsworth, 1969.

ISOCRATES. *Works*, trans. G. Norlin and L. van Hook. 3 vols. LCL, 1928–45. The most directly relevant works are 'Against the Sophists' and 'Antidosis' (both in vol. II).

LONGINUS. *On the Sublime*, in *Aristotle, Horace, Longinus: Classical Literary Criticism*, trans. T. S. Dorsch. Harmondsworth, 1965.

LUCIAN. 'A Professor of Public Speaking', in *Works*, vol. IV, trans. A. M. Harmon. LCL, 1925.

PLATO. *Gorgias*, in *Works*, vol. V, trans. W. R. M. Lamb. LCL, 1925.

Phaedrus, in *Works*, vol. I, trans. H. N. Fowler. LCL, 1914.

QUINTILIAN. *Institutio Oratoria*, trans. H. E. Butler. 4 vols. LCL, 1920–2.

Rhetorica ad Herennium, trans H. Caplan, LCL, 1954. Of unknown authorship; formerly attributed to Cicero.

(b) Studies

BOLGAR, R. R. *The Classical Heritage and its Beneficiaries*. Cambridge, 1954.

Brings out the central importance of rhetoric in classical and medieval education.

CURTIUS, ERNST ROBERT. *European Literature and the Latin Middle Ages*, trans. Willard R. Task. New York, 1953. First published 1948.

Especially chapters 4, 5, 8, 10: the prestige of rhetoric, the topics, poetry and rhetoric.

KENNEDY, GEORGE. *The Art of Persuasion in Greece*. Princeton and London, 1963.

Detailed and authoritative.

MOLINA, DAVID NEWTON-DE. Review of Herwig Blum, *Die antike Mnemotechnik* (1969), in *Essays in Criticism*, XX (1970), pp. 353–9.

A useful starting-point for anyone interested in the role of *memory* in traditional rhetoric.

MEDIEVAL RHETORIC

ATKINS, J. W. H. *English Literary Criticism: the Medieval Phase*. Cambridge, 1943.

Chapter 5, and appendix – a convenient summary of Geoffrey of Vinsauf's rhetorico-poetical doctrines.

TANENHAUS, GUSSIE H. 'Bede's *De Schematibus et Tropis* – a Translation', *The Quarterly Journal of Speech*, XLVIII (1962), pp. 237–53.

FROM THE RENAISSANCE TO THE ROMANTICS

(a) Texts

BLAIR, HUGH. *Lectures on Rhetoric and Belles Lettres*. 2 vols. London, 1783; reprinted, with an Introduction by Harold F. Harding, 2 vols. Carbondale and London, 1965.

(*The Rhetoric of Blair, Campbell, and Whately*, ed. James L. Golden and E. P. J. Corbett (New York, 1968) reprints selections from Blair's *Lectures*, George Campbell's *The Philosophy of Rhetoric* (1776), and Richard Whateley's *Elements of Rhetoric* (1828), with useful introductory essays.)

FRAUNCE, ABRAHAM. *The Arcadian Rhetorike* [1588], ed. Ethel Seaton. Oxford, 1950.

A work which 'combined the virtues of a useful textbook and an elegant anthology' (Introduction, p. li).

HOSKINS, JOHN. *Directions for Speech and Style* [ca. 1599], ed. Hoyt H. Hudson. Princeton, 1935.

Concise and pleasantly written.

PUTTENHAM, GEORGE. *The Arte of English Poesie*, ed. Gladys D. Willcock and Alice Walker. Cambridge, 1936; reprinted 1970.

Begun probably in the 1560s; first published 1589.

SIDNEY, SIR PHILIP. *An Apology for Poetry, or the Defence of Poesy* [1595], ed. Geoffrey Shepherd. London, 1965.

The editor's Introduction is full and illuminating.

SMITH, ADAM. *Lectures on Rhetoric and Belles Lettres*, ed. John M. Lothian. London, 1963.

The text of Smith's unpublished lectures, taken down by a student at Glasgow in 1762–3.

WILSON, THOMAS. *The Arte of Rhetorique* [2nd ed., 1560], ed. G. H. Mair. Oxford, 1909.

There is also a facsimile of the first edition (1553) with an introduction by R. H. Bowers (Gainesville, Florida, 1962).

(b) Studies

BALDWIN, THOMAS W. *William Shakspere's Small Latine and Lesse Greeke*. 2 vols. Urbana, Illinois, 1944.

School-rhetoric in sixteenth-century England, and its influence on Shakespeare.

BRADBROOK, M. C. *Themes and Conventions of Elizabethan Tragedy*. Cambridge, 1953. Chapters 4 and 5.

CLARK, DONALD L. *John Milton at St. Paul's School. A Study of*

Ancient Rhetoric in English Renaissance Education. New York, 1948.

CRAIG, HARDIN. *The Enchanted Glass: the Elizabethan Mind in Literature.* New York, 1936. Chapters 6 and 7.

CROLL, MORRIS W. *Style, Rhetoric, and Rhythm,* ed. J. Max Patrick and Robert O. Evans. Princeton, 1966.
A collection of essays dealing particularly with prose style in the sixteenth and seventeenth centuries.

HOWELL, WILBUR S. *Logic and Rhetoric in England, 1500–1700.* Princeton, 1956.

JOSEPH, BERTRAM L. *Elizabethan Acting.* London, 1951.
The influence of rhetorical delivery on acting styles.

SONNINO, LEE A. *A Handbook to Sixteenth-Century Rhetoric.* London, 1968.
A reference list of figures, genres, and aspects of style. The brief Introduction makes several interesting points.

STONE, P. W. K. *The Art of Poetry, 1750–1820.* London, 1967.
The downfall of a rhetoric-dominated theory of poetry.

TUVE, ROSEMOND. *Elizabethan and Metaphysical Imagery: Renaissance Poetic and Twentieth-Century Critics.* Chicago, 1947. Especially chapter 8.

THE TWENTIETH CENTURY

(a) Some general and theoretical studies

BOOTH, WAYNE C. *The Rhetoric of Fiction.* Chicago, 1961.

BROOKS, CLEANTH, and ROBERT PENN WARREN. *Modern Rhetoric.* 2nd ed. New York, 1958.
A course book for classroom use.

CROCE, BENEDETTO. *Aesthetic,* trans. Douglas Ainslie. 2nd ed. London, 1922. Especially part I, chapter 9, and part II, chapter 19, section i.

DAVIE, DONALD. 'Sixteenth-Century Poetry and the Common

Reader. The Case of Thomas Sackville', *Essays in Criticism*, IV (1954), pp. 117–27.

This essay led to an interesting exchange of views between Davie and J. B. Broadbent, with a postscript by F. W. Bateson (pp. 421–30).

ELIOT, T. S. '" Rhetoric" and Poetic Drama' [1919], in *Selected Essays*, 3rd ed. (London, 1951), pp. 37–42.

Also relevant are 'Shakespeare and the Stoicism of Seneca' and the essays on Marlowe and Ben Jonson.

LEECH, GEOFFREY N. *A Linguistic Guide to English Poetry*. London, 1969.

Amongst other things, a reappraisal of rhetoric in the light of linguistics.

LERNER, LAURENCE. *The Truest Poetry: An Essay on the Question What is Literature?* London, 1960. Chapter 3, 'Literature is Rhetoric'.

RICHARDS, I. A. *The Philosophy of Rhetoric*. New York and London, 1936.

WIMSATT, W. K. *The Verbal Icon*. Kentucky, 1954; London, 1970.

The Introduction and the essays on style in part 3 are of especial interest.

(b) Rhetoric in Criticism

Studies of the rhetorical forms and techniques used by individual authors are many and varied. What follows is a very brief selection, arranged chronologically according to the author who is being discussed. Fuller bibliographies will be found in Vickers, *Classical Rhetoric in English Poetry*, and in E. P. J. Corbett (ed.), *Rhetorical Analyses of Literary Works* (New York, 1969).

SHEPHERD, GEOFFREY, ed. *Ancrene Wisse (Parts Six and Seven)*. London, 1959. Introduction, pp. lix–lxxi.

STANLEY, E. G., ed. *The Owl and the Nightingale*. London, 1960. Introduction, pp. 25 ff.

PAYNE, ROBERT O. 'Chaucer and the Art of Rhetoric', in *Companion to Chaucer Studies*, ed. Beryl Rowland (Toronto, 1968), pp. 38–57.

A survey of writings in this field.

CLEMEN, WOLFGANG. *English Tragedy before Shakespeare: the Development of Dramatic Speech*, trans. T. S. Dorsch. London, 1961.

First published 1955; analyses the topics and structures of the set speech.

BARISH, JONAS A. '*The Spanish Tragedy*, or The Pleasures and Perils of Rhetoric', in *Elizabethan Theatre*, ed. J. R. Brown and Bernard Harris (Stratford-upon-Avon Studies, IX, London, 1966), pp. 58–85.

SMITH, HALLETT. *Elizabethan Poetry. A Study in Conventions, Meaning, and Expression*. Cambridge, Mass., 1952.

For Spenser, Shakespeare, and (above all) Sidney.

MYRICK, KENNETH O. *Sir Philip Sidney as a Literary Craftsman*. Cambridge, Mass., and London, 1935. Chapter 2: 'The *Defence of Poesie* as a Classical Oration.'

RINGLER, WILLIAM A., JR., ed. *The Poems of Sir Philip Sidney*. Oxford, 1962. Introduction: Sidney and rhetoric.

VICKERS, BRIAN. *Francis Bacon and Renaissance Prose*. Cambridge, 1968. Chapters 2 and 4.

MIRIAM JOSEPH, SISTER. *Shakespeare's Use of the Arts of Language*. New York, 1947. Thorough but unexciting.

VICKERS, BRIAN. *The Artistry of Shakespeare's Prose*. London, 1968.

Chapter 2, and valuable comments on individual plays, e.g. *The Merchant of Venice* (pp. 82–7), *As You Like It* (pp. 217–19), *Julius Caesar* (pp. 241 ff.), and *Measure for Measure* (pp. 320 ff.).

FRANCE, PETER. *Racine's Rhetoric*. Oxford, 1965.

Examines the presence in Racine's work of 'two different sorts of rhetoric, the functional and the decorative'.

BROADBENT, J. B. 'Milton's Rhetoric', *Modern Philology*, LVI (1959), pp. 224–42. Reprinted in Alan Rudrum (ed.), *Milton: Modern Judgments* (London, 1968).

FEDER, LILLIAN. 'John Dryden's Use of Classical Rhetoric', *P.M.L.A.*, LXIX (1954), pp. 1258–78. Reprinted in H. T. Swedenberg (ed.), *Essential Articles for the Study of John Dryden* (New York and London, 1966), pp. 493–518.

MAURER, A. E. W. 'The Structure of Dryden's *Astraea Redux*', *Papers on Language and Literature*, II (1966), pp. 13–20.

OLSON, ELDER. 'Rhetoric and the Appreciation of Pope', *Modern Philology*, XXXVII (1939–40), pp. 13–35. Reprinted in Corbett, *Rhetorical Analyses*.

PETRIE, GRAHAM. 'Rhetoric as Fictional Technique in *Tristram Shandy*', *Philological Quarterly*, XLVIII (1969), pp. 479–94.

BOULTON, JAMES T. *The Language of Politics in the Age of Wilkes and Burke*. London, 1963.

SUCKSMITH, H. P. *The Narrative Art of Charles Dickens: the Rhetoric of Sympathy and Irony in his Novels*. London, 1970.
In Dickens' case, the rhetoric of fiction is 'the technical means whereby, through structure, effects are created and vision focused' (p. 7).

HOLLOWAY, JOHN. *The Victorian Sage: Studies in Argument*. London, 1953.
Especially for Carlyle, Newman, and Arnold.

Index

Library
Canterbury High School
Ottawa